YASO HANAMURA

ANIMETA!

03

Meet the Cast

Inspired by the anime that taught her what it means to be truly passionate about something, nineteen-year-old Miyuki Sanada finds herself on the steps of a prominent anime studio. She's excited to see her own drawings come to life, but she's having a hard time getting better! And everyone's always yelling at her! But what really takes the cake is the fact that if she doesn't take the key animation exam within the year, she's fired! Where will Yukimura's love, effort, and hardship-filled anime journey take her?!

Protagonist

Miyuki Sanada

A rookie animator and the protagonist of this series. Her skills aren't quite there yet, but her strong intuition landed her a job at N2 Factory Studio. She's been improving little by little thanks to her dedication to the job and her love for anime. She adores N2's "Royal Girl Pannacotta" with all her heart. Her nickname is Yukimura.

Maria Date

One of Yukimura's colleagues who joined the studio at the same time. Her mother is a famous manga artist, but she doesn't talk about that very much. Maria immediately makes a name for herself with hard work and her inherited talent. She doesn't have very fond feelings about Yukimura, who Kujo seems to be giving special treatment.

Yuiko Fuji

An inbetween checker at N2's Studio 2, and Yukimura's mentor. She's extremely skilled at her job. She seems to harbor complicated feelings about Kujo.

Kujo

The director of N2's Studio 7. He served as assistant director on Pannacotta. Not only does he have a profound love of animation, but he bets his very life on his work. Yukimura's instincts may have garnered her favor with him, but he's that much stricter with her as a result.

Kanjiya

The assistant director of N2's Studio 7. He's Director Kujo's right-hand man. His nickname is Gandhi. He has a daughter that he loves very much.

Igarashi

An unparalleled animator at N2's Studio 7. He was the animation director on episode 12 of Pannacotta. He hits the bottle a little harder than he probably should.

N2's President

President of N2 Factory Studio. He gave Miyuki the nickname "Yukimura". Historically, everyone he's given a nickname has quit.

Kitagawa

One of N2's production assistants. He manages the schedule and budget of productions. He's a very capable production assistant, who will use any means necessary to get things done.

Asaishi

A key animator at N2's Studio 2. He's Maria's mentor, and despite her outward attitude, he can tell she's a hard worker.

Natou

A new animator at N2 who at the same time as Yukimura. He was the vice president of his college's animation club. He's a little full of himself.

ANIMETA!

YASO HANAMURA 03

*Key Animation (Genga): The process of drawing the images that become the *key* moments of motion. The term used in the Japanese industry to describe keyframes, genga, literally means "original drawings" because the "original" drawings of the key animators are ultimately traced and cleaned by the inbetweeners, becoming douga, before they are finalized.

ガチャッ
TCHK!

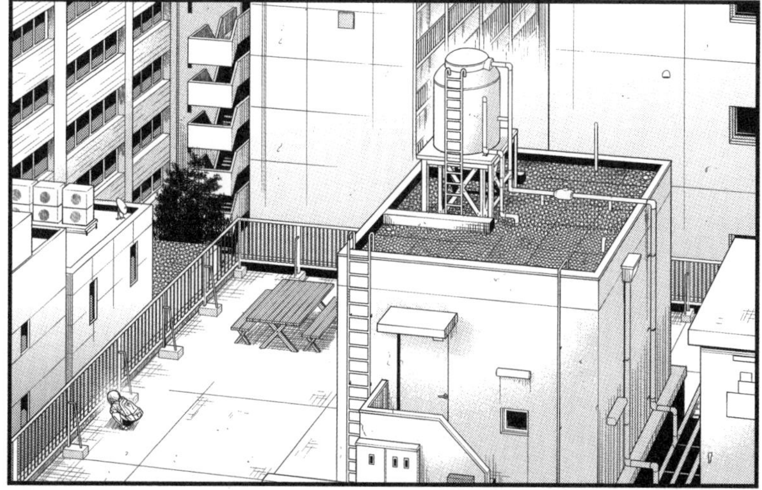

...sa,
djip'talou

うっ
Squeeze
ぎゅ
sob...
Solin, soli'sa, djip'talou
Solin, soli'sa, djip'talou
Solin, soli'sa, djip'talou

スクッ
Fwoosh
OKAY!

ガチャ
KTCHK!
STUDIO 2

UM...
YES?

HERE... I MADE A COPY OF THOSE SAIBANE FRAMES YOU WANTED, ARE YOU STILL INTERESTED?
I AM! THANK YOU SO MUCH!

Wow!

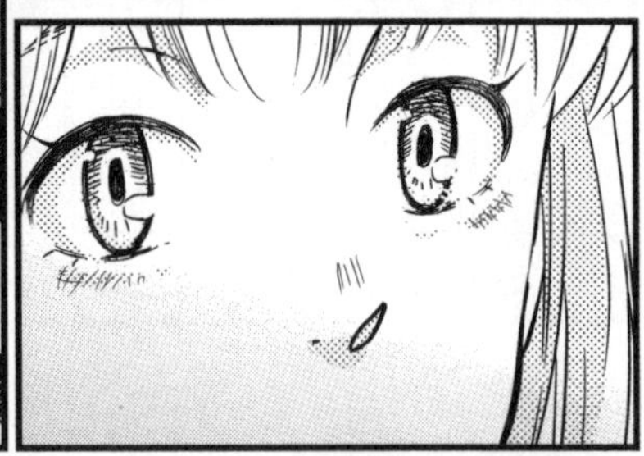

ENOUGH CHIT-CHAT, GET TO WORK.

HERE.

YES, MA'AM.

5

Do Marimo Count As Pets?

3/5

IT'S FROM "MARIPET"... WAIT, ISN'T EPISODE FOUR AIRING TODAY?

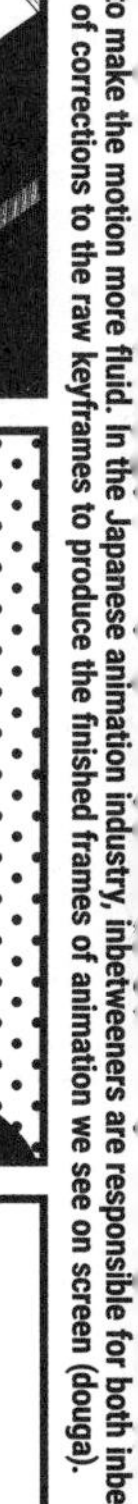
frames *between* keyframes to make the motion more fluid. In the Japanese animation industry, inbetweeners are responsible for both inbetweening and the cleaning and application of corrections to the raw keyframes to produce the finished frames of animation we see on screen (douga).

ARE TV SERIES USUALLY THIS DOWN-TO-THE-WIRE?
THERE ARE SOME RARE EXCEPTIONS WHERE A PRODUCTION HAS ROOM TO BREATHE, BUT EVEN MOVIES TEND TO BE A RACE AGAINST THE CLOCK.

YOUR DEADLINE IS MONDAY, SO YOU'VE GOT TWO DAYS.
Y-YES, MA'AM!
5
Do Marimo Count As Pets?
C 3/5

I'M OFF FOR THE NIGHT.
GRUMBLE...
GRUMBLE...
...
Flip...
Flip...

...
OH...
MAYBE THIS IS IT?
GRUMBLE...
GRUMBLE...

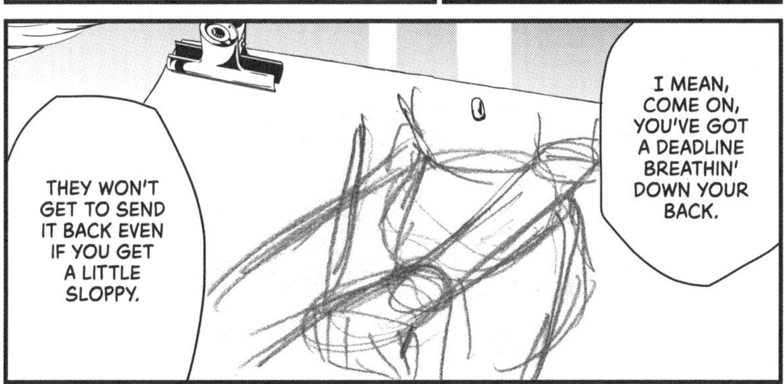

Sign: Tengu no Nukeana

A KAHLUA AND MILK.
AOJIRU FOR ME.

I'LL HAVE THE HAKKAISAN SAKE.
WE CAN'T SERVE ALCOHOL TO MINORS...
ID
AHEM!

She's 30...?
...

THEY'RE NOT A FAMILY?!
MOM
DAD
DAUGHTER
TH-THANK YOU FOR YOUR ORDER.

LOOK, LET'S JUST CUT TO THE CHASE. DID SOMETHING HAPPEN?
YOU DON'T USUALLY INVITE US OUT TO DRINK.

WHAT'S TWEENING BY THE BOOK, ANYWAY?
ガサ RUSTLE...
ガサ RUSTLE...
WHAT KIND OF TWEENS IS HE DRAWING?
パラ FLIP
パラ FLIP
パラ FLIP
パラ FLIP
HM...?
パラ FLIP
パラ FLIP
UGH... THE MOTION'S REALLY FLAT.
I WONDER WHY IT LOOKS LIKE THAT.
ガサ RUSTLE...
ガサ RUSTLE...
LET'S SEE WHAT MARIA'S WORK LOOKS LIKE.

SHE BARELY DOES ANY CONSTRUCTION AT ALL...?
HM...
IS THAT WHY SHE'S SO FAST?
STUDIO

23:45
HOLD ON!
I DON'T HAVE TIME TO LOOK AT OTHER PEOPLE'S WORK!
森の記憶
修正集

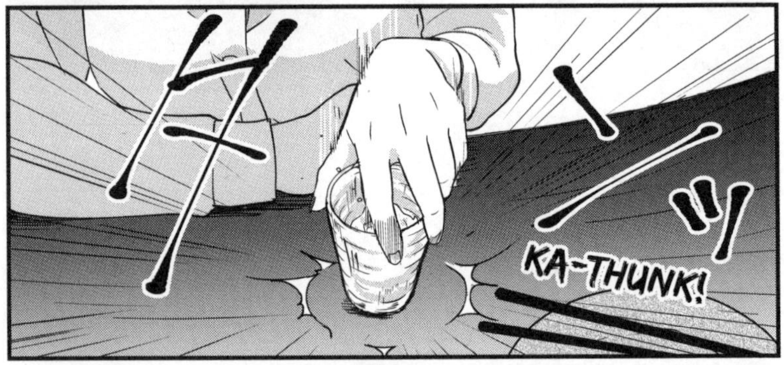
KA-THUNK!

I MEAN, ACTING LIKE DRAWING 500 FRAMES IN A MONTH IS NOTHING IS NUTS!
IT STOPPED BEING REALISTIC OVER 30 YEARS AGO!

GLUG
GLUG
IN THE DAYS OF YORE, PRODUCING ROUGHER WORK WAS MUCH MORE PERMISSIBLE.

NOW, I KNOW THIS IS ONLY MY NINTH YEAR AT N2,
BUT I'VE ONLY EVER SEEN TWO PEOPLE MOVE UP TO KEY ANIMATION IN THEIR FIRST YEAR!
AND YOU PERSONALLY TRAINED BOTH OF THEM, DIDN'T YOU?
GIVE YOURSELF SOME MORE CREDIT, TEACH!
だし巻き玉子
450
BUT...
THOSE TWO WERE ALREADY EXTREMELY TALENTED.
ALL I CAN TEACH ANYONE IS HOW TO TWEEN.

ぐすっ
Sniffle...
ぐすっ
Sniffle...
HUH?!
WHY'RE YOU CRYIN'?!

SoftBank 3G
92%
Edit

ぐすっ
Sniffle...
ぐすっ
Sniffle...
I miss my little Mii...
SHE'S JUST AT YOUR PARENTS' FOR GOLDEN WEEK.

ぐすっ
Sniffle...
ぐすっ
Sniffle...
NOT YOU TOO!

I GOT REJECTED!
Remilio
"I consider you a good friend, Yuiko, and I don't want to change our relationship..."

Asagaya Station
I can't believe even 2D men are dumping me... There really is no love in this world...
DRINK.
TUMERIC POWER
Mii...
I love you, Tama!
YEAH, YEAH. NOW SIT DOWN AND DRINK THIS.

I HATE THIS BENCH.
WHY?

HE SAYS HE'S NOT WAITING THREE YEARS!
SO SHE'S FIRED IF SHE DOESN'T PASS THE KEY ANIMATOR EXAM IN A YEAR!
I don't get it!

DID... MR. KUJO SAY THAT?
HE DID.

HM...
WAIT, HE'S NOT...

THE SUN'S STINGING MY EYES...

UGGGH... I'M SO TIRED...

ヨロ
WOBBLE

ヨロ
WOBBLE

IF SHE DOESN'T PASS THE KEY ANIMATION EXAM WITHIN A YEAR, SHE'S FIRED.

FILL A SKETCH-BOOK...
CROQUIS
IN TEN DAYS.
...I HAVE TO DRAW.
...

WAIT...

WHAT EXACTLY DOES "DRAW EVERYTHING YOU SEE" MEAN?

Shk
シャッ
Shk
シャッ
Shk
シャッ
Shk
シャッ
Shk
シャッ
Shk
シャッ
Shk
シャッ
Shk
シャッ
Shk
シャッ
Shk
シャッ
Shk
シャッ
Shk
シャッ

Growl!
ギュルルルルル
緑豆
もやし
Bag: Bean Sprouts

RIGHT...
YOU'RE ALL I HAVE LEFT...
節約

...HMPH!
RUSTLE RUSTLE
EXTRA VEGGIES!
太麺
豚キムチ
キムチ入り
ラーメン
BUTAKIMU

SHHHHH!

Shk
Shk

Tick
Tick
Tick

Shk
Shk
BEEF TONGUE ♡
BBQ RIBS (TOP QUALITY)
A5 RANK
BLACK WAGYUU
YUKHOE

うっとり
SPACED OUT

Klunk
BUTAKIMU
ALRIGHT.
パンナコッタ

N2 FACTORY STUDIO

REDO IT.
Wibble
Wobble

WHAT'S WRONG?

OH... NOTHING. I'LL REDO IT...

I WON'T HAVE TIME TO EAT DINNER AT THIS RATE.

GRAB!
ガッ
眠気スッキリ爽快!!
BLACK
Bottle: Energy in a bottle!
ザラ ザラ
SHAKE
SHAKE
ザラ ザラ
SHAKE
SHAKE
Hnnngh!
THERE WE GO!
ボリ ボリ ボリ
CRUNCH
CRUNCH
CRUNCH
YOU BARELY GOT IT IN BY THE DEADLINE AGAIN... STILL, GOOD JOB, I GUESS.
I... I'm sorry.
M2 FACTORY STUDIO
...I DID IT!

...AS A KEY ANIMATOR ON YOUR NEXT PRODUCTION, ARE YOU?

...

...TEN DAYS.

WHAT?
I TOLD HER TO FILL A SKETCHBOOK IN TEN DAYS.

KTCHK!
ガチャッ
BUT...
A NEW INBETWEENER ISN'T GOING TO HAVE TIME FOR...
EXCUSE ME!

CROQUIS
100sheets maruman
HERE.
I FILLED THE WHOLE THING, SO PLEASE TAKE A LOOK!
CROQUIS
パラ
FLIP...
パラ
FLIP
パラ
FLIP
パラ
FLIP
パラ
FLIP

YOU WEREN'T EXACTLY WRONG,
BUT YOU WEREN'T EXACTLY RIGHT EITHER.
...
I UNDERSTAND. I'LL TRY AGAIN.
THANK YOU VERY MUCH.
EXCUSE ME.
CROQUI
IT'S PRETTY AMAZING THAT SHE MANAGED TO DO THAT IN JUST TEN DAYS.
NO, SHE PROBABLY DID IT IN ONE DAY.

WHAT?!
TNK!
CHECK-MATE.
WAIT, WHAT?
Use your whol
arm to draw
long lines
Don't give up!

Shk
Shk
Shk
Shk
500 frames in one month

Shk
Shk
Shk

STUDIO 2

MAKO, BUDDY...

I MIGHT NOT HAVE THIS READY IN AN HOUR.
DON'T WORRY! I BELIEVE IN YOU!

SOLIN, SOLI'SA, DJIP' TALOU!
SHINE!
NO, SERIOUSLY, IT'S NOT HAPPENING.

UM,
I'D LIKE YOU TO TAKE A LOOK AT MY WORK, PLEASE.

パラ FLIP
パラ FLIP
パラ FLIP
パラ FLIP
パラ FLIP

OKAY, LOOKS GOOD TO ME.
IMPRES-SIVE AS ALWAYS.
EVEN THE PRODUCTION SECTION THINKS YOU'RE THE BEST NEW INBETWEENER WE'VE HIRED IN YEARS.

...
WHAT WAS THAT SPELL, OR WHATEVER, YOU SAID EARLIER?

OH...

SOLIN, SOLI'SA, DJIP'TALOU?

"IF YOU BELIEVE, AND KEEP PUSHING FORWARD, A PATH WILL OPEN BEFORE YOU."
...IS WHAT IT'S SUPPOSED TO MEAN.
IT'S A LINE FROM PANNA-COTTA, AND...
FAS-CINAT-ING.
...
EXCUSE ME, PLEASE.
...WELL,
I GUESS SHE PROBABLY DOESN'T NEED TO HEAR THOSE WORDS, HUH?
SHE'S SO YOUNG AND HER WORK IS ALREADY INCREDIBLE.
PLUS, HER MOTHER'S A FAMOUS MANGA ARTIST. SHE MUST BE RICH, RIGHT?

SHE ALREADY HAS A BRIGHT FUTURE AHEAD OF HER.

SIGN: NO PARKING WITHIN COMPLEX
団地内
駐車禁止

2-109
DATE

ガチャッ
KTCHK!
2

MOM, I'M HOME...

カチャ CLACK
カチャ CLACK
カチャ CLACK
カチャ CLACK

Manga Cover: Maison de Android
Kiraru Date

...SO WILL YOU GO BACK TO DRAWING MANGA LIKE YOU USED TO IF I MAKE IT HAPPEN?

カチャ CLACK カチャ CLACK カチャ CLACK カチャ CLACK カチャ CLACK カチャ CLACK カチャ CLACK カチャ CLACK カチャ CLACK カチャ CLACK

CHAPTER 12: HER MEMORIES

DID YOU DRAW THIS?
OH NO, MARIA DEAR,
IF MANGA ARTISTS HAD TO DRAW THE ANIME, THEY'D DIE.

?
HUH? SO THOSE ARE MOM'S DRAWINGS, BUT SHE DIDN'T DRAW THEM HERSELF?
THE PICTURES THAT MAKE UP ANIME AREN'T DRAWN BY THE MANGA ARTISTS,
BUT BY PEOPLE CALLED ANIMATORS.

ANI... MATORS?

YES.
THEY'RE ARTISTS WHO SPECIALIZE IN MAKING DRAWINGS MOVE.

ACTUALLY, BACK BEFORE I BECAME AN ASSISTANT, I WAS AN ANIMATOR.
REALLY?! YOU NEVER MENTIONED IT.
I THOUGHT IT'D BE THE PERFECT JOB FOR ME, SINCE IT INVOLVED DRAWING EVERY DAY...
BUT I DIDN'T HAVE THE DRAWING ABILITY OR TALENT FOR IT, SO I ENDED UP QUITTING.

NOT EVEN YOU COULD HANDLE IT, CHIEF OOMORI?
OF COURSE NOT.

IN THE PROFESSIONAL WORLD, ENTHUSIASM MEANS NOTHING.
IF YOU DON'T HAVE THE SKILLS TO BACK IT UP, IT'S ALL WORTHLESS.
BUT YOU MADE IT TO CHIEF ASSISTANT RIGHT AFTER YOU GOT INTO MANGA, DIDN'T YOU?
EXACTLY. I LIKED DRAWING, BUT I WASN'T ANY GOOD AT MAKING THINGS MOVE.
THE EXPERIENCE MADE ME REALIZE I PREFERRED TAKING MY TIME ON STILL ILLUSTRATIONS.

WELL, I DID GET THE BASICS OF PERSPECTIVE AND STUFF BEATEN INTO ME WHEN I WAS TRYING TO BE AN ANIMATOR, SO THAT HELPED.

HEY, IT'S STARTING!

WHAT IS WITH THOSE CLOTHES? THEY'RE HIDEOUS.

...
AND THE COLORS ARE AWFUL.
ブツ Mumble...
ブツ Mumble...

THIS IS WHY I SAID I WANTED N2...

MOM?
スクッ Shnk

KTHNK

WHAT'S WRONG WITH MOM?

WELL ...

SHE'S A BIT OF A PERFECTIONIST...
I GUESS THE ANIME JUST ISN'T UP TO HER STANDARDS.

GETTING AN ANIME ADAPTATION IS A MASSIVE ACCOMPLISHMENT, BUT SHE PROBABLY WANTED IT TO BE PERFECT, SINCE THE OPPORTUNITIES ARE SO FEW AND FAR BETWEEN.

THOUGH, IT'S HONESTLY IMPOSSIBLE TO MAKE SOMETHING THAT MATCHES UP ENTIRELY WITH THE CREATOR'S VISION.
ANIME AND MANGA ARE COMPLETELY DIFFERENT ANIMALS, SO THEY HAVE TO BE TACKLED DIFFERENTLY.

HUH?
SO, MOM ISN'T HAPPY ABOUT THE ANIME?
I don't get it.

HMM... I WOULDN'T SAY SHE'S UNHAPPY, BUT...

WELL, LET'S JUST SAY IF YOU WANNA IMPRESS HER,
YOU'VE GOTTA PRODUCE SOMETHING A LOT BETTER THAN THIS.

Shk

Shk
Shk

YOU REALLY ARE GOOD AT DRAWING, MARIA.
I WANT TO BE AN ANIMATOR WHEN I GROW UP.
THEN, I CAN MAKE AN ANIME THAT'LL MAKE YOU PROUD, MOM!
...WILL YOU, NOW?
THEN I GUESS I'LL JUST HAVE TO WORK HARD AT DRAWING MANGA.
BUT REAL-ITY...
...WAS NOT SO KIND.

ARE YOU READING KIRARU DATE'S LATEST SERIES?
HER SERIES THAT HAD BEEN ADAPTED INTO AN ANIME ENDED.
NO, IT WAS BORING, SO I DROPPED IT. "ITSUKOI" IS ALL THE RAGE RIGHT NOW, RIGHT?

カチャ CLACK!
カチャ CLACK!
SHE SLOWLY STOPPED DRAWING.
AND EVENTUALLY, SHE WITHDREW ENTIRELY INTO HER SHELL.
カチャ CLACK!
カチャ CLACK!
カチャ CLACK!
カチャ CLACK!
カチャ CLACK!
カチャ CLACK!
NO ONE WANTS ME ANYMORE...
ULTIMATELY, SHE QUIT MAKING MANGA.
カチャ CLACK!
カチャ CLACK!
ピ BEEP!
ピ BEEP!
ピ BEEP!
ピ BEEP!

BEEP!
BEEP!
BEEP!
BEEP!
...I HAVE TO GET TO WORK.
N2 FACTORY STUDIO
GOOD MORNING.
STUDIO 2
WH...
WHAT'S THAT?!

Total Frames for 4/1 - 4/30
Azuma 492
Makimura 380
Yunoshima 461
Katou 375
Iwanami 197
Oobayashi 520
Harimaya 173
Fuji 355
Totsuka 440
Sanada 0
Date 256
Natou 168
Kashiwa 487
Kai 449
Kasagi 429
Sonomiya 371
Kajio 156
Shinozaki 194
Masaka 320
0 100 200 300 400 500
IT'S A CHART OF HOW MANY FRAMES ALL OUR INBETWEENERS HAVE DRAWN IN THE PAST MONTH.
H... HOW TERRIFY-ING...
AND IT'S RIGHT UP ON THE DOOR...
IT'S LIKE A PUBLIC EXECUTION!
I KNOW HOW YOU FEEL. I WAS RATHER SLOW MYSELF, SO I NEVER RACKED UP PARTICULARLY IMPRESSIVE NUMBERS.
YOU WERE SLOW TOO, MR. ASAISHI?

IF SHE DOESN'T PASS THE KEY ANIMATION EXAM WITHIN A YEAR, SHE'S FIRED.

HOW RUDE.
DO I LOOK LIKE A MON-STER?
I'M NOT REALLY SURE WHAT ELSE TO CALL SOMEONE WHO HOVERS OVER MY SHOULDER UNTIL I TURN IN A CUT...
WHY DON'T WE TRY "EXCELLENT PRODUCTION ASSISTANT" INSTEAD?
OH, THE MONTHLY TOTALS ARE UP.
THAT ONE PRETTY GIRL IS REALLY IMPRESSIVE.
Katou
Iwanami
Oobayashi
Harimaya
Fuji
Totsuka
Sanada
Date
Natou
Kashiwa
Kai
Kasagi
Sonomiya
440
0
256
300
SHE WAS STILL IN TRAINING IN APRIL, BUT SHE MANAGED TO FINISH 256 FRAMES!
...BUT ON THE OTHER HAND, THE STUDIO 7 NEWBIE DID A WHOPPING ZERO.
YOU GOT REAL LUCKY WITH YOUR NEWBIE.
STUDIO 2

THE THING IS, TWEENING'S* A SKILL THAT NEEDS TO BE DEVELOPED.

IT'S NOT THE SORT OF THING YOU CAN EXCEL AT WITHOUT PRIOR KNOWLEDGE AND TRAINING.

THE FACT THAT SHE'S SO GOOD DESPITE BEING NEW AT THE JOB MUST MEAN...

Tweening (Nakawari): The process of adding frames between keyframes to make the animation move smoothly. In Japan, both tracing and cleaning the raw keyframes (genga) and the actual work of drawing inbetweens (nakawari) to produce the finalized animation frames (douga) are part of an inbetweener's job. Although the terms tweening and inbetweening are largely interchangeable in English, for clarity we'll be using "tweening" to describe only the actual process of drawing the inbetween frames (nakawari).

...SHE'S BEEN WORKING EXTRA HARD TO REFINE HER SKILLS.

*Inbetween Check (Douga Kensa, sometimes abbreviated to Douken): The job of ensuring that the inbetweens are neat and the motion smooth. Similar to the job of the Animation Director (sakuga kantoku) but for inbetweens and cleanup rather than key animation.

HM?
DID SOMETHING HAPPEN?

?
NO, NOTHING.
EXCUSE ME.

GOOD MORNING.
OH, MORNING.

HERE, I'D LIKE YOU TO HANDLE THIS, MARIA.
IT'S A LITTLE COMPLICATED, BUT DO YOU THINK YOU CAN TAKE CARE OF IT?
FLIP... FLIP...

IT WON'T BE A PROBLEM.
GOOD, THEN I'LL LEAVE IT TO YOU.

I FIGURED COMPLETING ZERO FRAMES WAS NORMAL, SINCE WE'RE STILL IN TRAINING AND ALL,
SO HOW'D SHE FINISH 256 REAL, PRODUCTION FRAMES?

SHE BARELY DOES ANY SKETCHING, TOO...
Shk シャカ
Shk
Shk シャカ
Shk シャカ
I WONDER HOW SHE BREAKS DOWN THE MOTION.
Shk シャカ

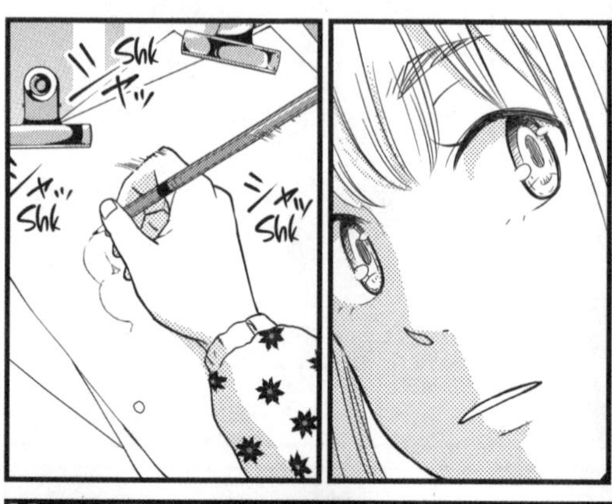
Shk
Shk
Shk

MS. FUJI, YOU DON'T SKETCH MUCH EITHER, DO YOU?
HM?
OH, THIS IS THE SORT OF CUT WHERE SHIFT AND TRACE IS MORE THAN SUFFICIENT.
I DO UNDER-DRAWINGS FOR MORE COMPLICATED CUTS.

YOU DO?
太麺
豚キムチ
ラーメン

DON'T TELL ME YOU'VE BEEN ROUGHING OUT ALL YOUR TWEENS...
I HAVE.

Shift and Trace

HMM...

THIS IS DRASTICALLY OVERSIMPLIFYING, BUT IF YOU HAVE A CUT WITHOUT A LOT OF CHANGES IN ANGLE, OR ONE WHERE ALL THE MOVEMENT IS IN A SINGLE PLANE,

Looking up

Hand waving from side to side

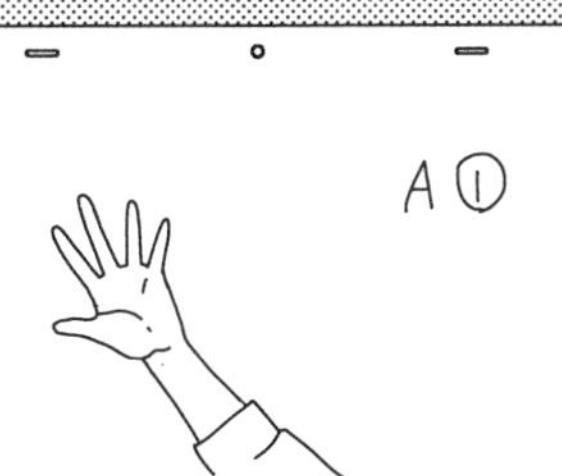

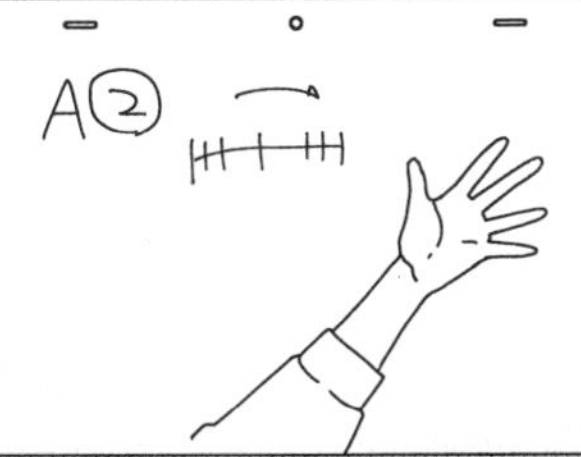

YOU CAN USE THE SHIFT AND TRACE TECHNIQUE I DESCRIBED BEFORE TO TWEEN WITHOUT ANY UNDERDRAWINGS.

Constructed Tweens

BUT SIMILARLY, IF YOU USE SHIFT AND TRACE ON A SEQUENCE THAT REQUIRES A MORE CONSTRUCTED APPROACH,
THE MOTION WILL BE OFF AND THE IMAGE WILL BE RUINED.

SO HOW DO YOU DETERMINE WHEN A SET OF KEYFRAMES IS GOOD ENOUGH TO GET AWAY WITH SHIFT AND TRACE?
THE ONLY WAY TO LEARN IS BY DOING. AND DOING A LOT.

...
I GUESS THERE REALLY ISN'T ANY OTHER WAY...

STUDIO 7

KITA-
GAWA.
YES? WHAT DO YOU NEED?

DELIVER THIS CUT TO THE STUDIO 7 NEWBIE.
WILL DO.

THOUGH, ON THAT NOTE, THAT EXPLOSION CUT YOU HAD MS. SANADA HANDLE EARLIER...
ENDED UP BEING ALMOST ENTIRELY CORRECTED BY MS. FUJI, DIDN'T IT?

OF COURSE SHE COULDN'T TWEEN THAT CUT.
I GAVE IT TO HER TO TEACH HER A LESSON.
CROQUIS
100she
ONCE YOU FIGURE OUT WHAT YOU CAN'T DO AND WHAT YOU'RE LACKING,
WHAT YOU NEED TO DO BECOMES APPARENT.
Key Animation Exam Within A Year
500 frames in one month

Draw lines until the paper turns black!
Key Animation Exam Within A Year
500 frames in one month
THE MOST IMPORTANT THING FOR HER RIGHT NOW...
...IS TO DRAW A LOT AND IMPROVE HER SKILLS AS FAST AS POSSIBLE.
BUT CAN YOU REALLY IMPROVE THAT QUICKLY?
OF COURSE NOT.

PERSONALLY, AS A PRODUCTION ASSISTANT, I'M NOT INTERESTED IN WHETHER HIS TRAINING METHODS ARE EFFECTIVE.
NOT WHEN HIRING SOMEONE ALREADY COMPETENT SEEMS A LOT MORE PRACTICAL.
N2 FACTORY STUDIO
MY 35TH DAY AT N2.
I MEAN, IT'S GOLDEN WEEK. MIGHT AS WELL TAKE A BREAK, RIGHT?
YOU'VE GOT TIME TO SPARE WITH THE DEADLINE FOR THIS CUT.
FLIP パラ FLIP パラ
FLIP パラパラ FLIP
Well...
SURE, BUT I'M SLOW ENOUGH AS IT IS. PLUS, I WON'T MAKE ANY MONEY WHILE I'M ON BREAK...
GOOD POINT.
NOW REDO THIS.
HUH?

HONEY, I'M HOME!
HERE, HAVE SOME CUTS WE'D LIKE STUDIO 2 TO HANDLE.
GOT IT.
AND...
WELL, THIS IS A LITTLE PRESENT FOR MS. SANADA FROM DIRECTOR KUJO.
Title
(Film) Karisome
1 + 12
181
チェック
TP
スキャン
解像度
原画
動画
UM...

DON'T WORRY, IT'S AN EASY CUT.

R...

REALLY?

WHAT KIND OF CUT IS IT?

A 51 FRAME EFFECT* CUT THAT'S ALMOST FULL KEY ANIMATION*.

OOOH! NOW THAT'S A CUT!

Effects: Things like explosions, smoke, water, and light that enhance the image on screen.

Solo Cut / Full Key Animation: A cut in which both the keyframes and tweens are drawn by the key animator. They do not require additional tweens from an inbetweener, so it's the best option for cuts animators want to give particular attention to. However, it's a lot of work.

IT'S PROBABLY BECAUSE THE LAST ONE HE GAVE HER WAS SUCH A DOOZY.

THAT'S ANOTHER CUT FROM ONE OF STUDIO 7'S FILMS, ISN'T IT?

WHY ARE YOU LETTING MIYUKI, WHOSE WORK ALWAYS NEEDS TO BE REDONE, HELP ON A FILM PROJECT?
WHY NOT LET ME TAKE IT INSTEAD?

HMM...
TYPICALLY, WHEN WE RECEIVE CUTS TO TWEEN, THEY COME FROM THE VARIOUS SUB-STUDIOS AND GO TO WHOEVER IS IN CHARGE OF ASSIGNING THE WORK.
AND, ON THAT NOTE, I'M THE PERSON IN CHARGE OF ASSIGNING CUTS TO TWEEN AT STUDIO 2.

Title (Film) Karisome

THE CUTS THAT COME TO STUDIO 2 FOR TWEENING AND CLEANUP GET ASSIGNED TO STUDIO 2'S INBETWEENERS, OF COURSE,

BUT AS A GENERAL RULE, A NEWBIE WON'T EVER BE ASSIGNED A CUT FROM A FILM.

THAT SAID, YUKIMURA IS TECHNICALLY ATTACHED TO STUDIO 7, AND THE DIRECTOR HAS GIVEN HIS EXPRESS PERMISSION, SO THAT'S WHY SHE CAN WORK ON IT.

SO, YOU'RE SAYING...

IF I WERE ATTACHED TO STUDIO 7, THERE WOULDN'T BE AN ISSUE?

Rustle
Rustle

CROQUIS
FOR TRAINING RUN
GRAB

HEY, WHERE DO YOU THINK YOU'RE GOING?
スタ TAP
スタ TAP

EXCUSE ME.

CAN YOU PLEASE TAKE A LOOK AT THIS?

...
CROQUIS

I CAN...

SO PLEASE,

LET ME JOIN STUDIO 7 IN HER PLACE!

Let's Talk About Timing Charts and Frame Count

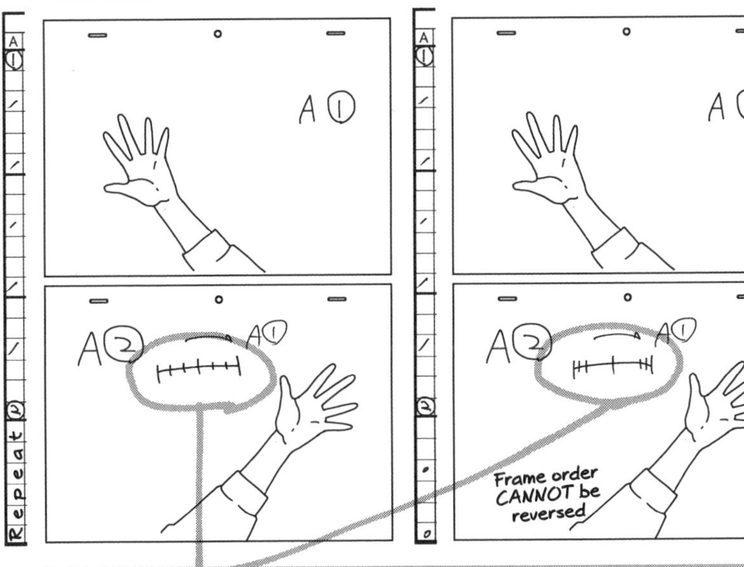

Timing Charts These are instructions for the inbetweener that explain how to space frames while tweening

- If the tweens don't follow the instructions of the timing chart, the motion won't match what the key animator was imagining.
- A cut tweened with exactly the same frame count, but different timing charts, can produce wildly different impressions in terms of acting, implications, speed, and weight (among other things).
- For example, even with the same key frames, the cut on the right with only one tween would end up looking like a much faster motion than either of the examples above.

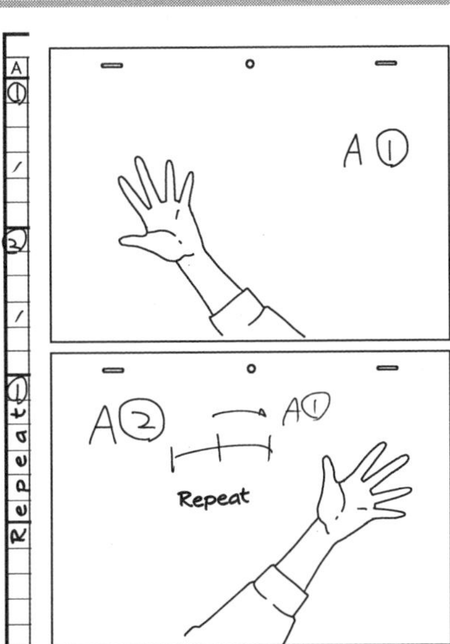

Figure 1

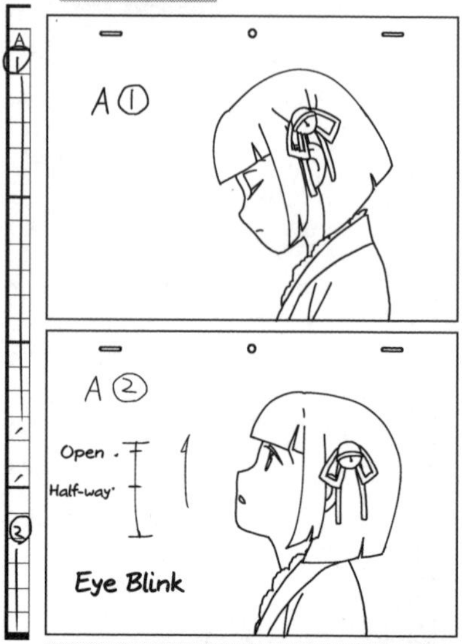

A ①

A ②

Open

Half-way

Eye Blink

Suddenly looking up

Figure 2

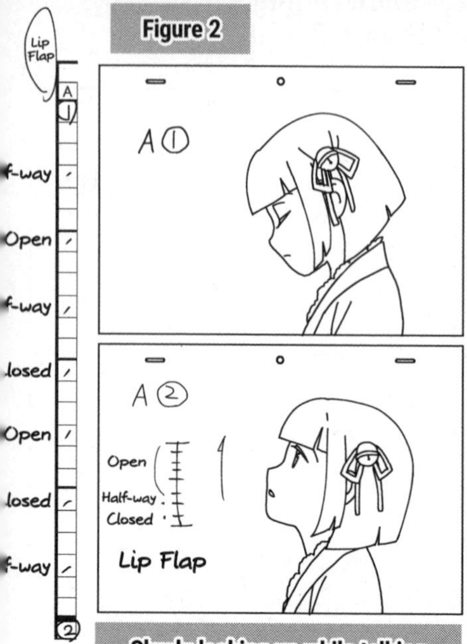

Lip Flap

f-way

Open

f-way

losed

Open

losed

f-way

A ①

A ②

Open

Half-way

Closed

Lip Flap

Slowly looking up while talking

- **Figure 1 uses four frames for a fast motion, but Figure 2 uses 24 for a slower one. Despite having the same keyframes, just changing the number of tweens can drastically alter the impression of a cut.**

- **"Eye Blinks" are added during the tweening process by creating frames with the eyes open, closed, and half-open.**

- **"Lip Flaps" are also added during the tweening process by moving the character's mouth.**

- **The more tweens required, the harder the work is for the inbetweener.**

Manga Cover: Maison de Android
Kiraru Date

SO PLEASE LET ME JOIN STUDIO 7.

CHAPTER 13: HALF A SECOND OF ETERNITY

FOR TRAINING PURPOSES
RUN

ペラ
FLIP
ペラ
FLIP
ペラ
FLIP

ポリ
CRUNCH
ポリ
CRUNCH

...I'M NOT IMPRESSED.

パラ
FLIP
パラ
FLIP
パラ
FLIP
パラ
FLIP
YOUR STILL ILLUSTRATIONS ARE DECENT ENOUGH, BUT THERE'S NO PLACE FOR YOU IN STUDIO 7.
GO BACK TO STUDIO 2.
CROQUIS
BUT...
EXCUSE ME, MS. DATE!

WHAT DO YOU THINK YOU'RE DOING HERE?!
SHE CAME TO PERSONALLY REQUEST TO JOIN STUDIO 7.

YOU—
OF COURSE YOU CAN'T!

WHY NOT?!
AT N2, YOU HAVE TO BE WORKING AS A KEY ANIMATOR FOR AT LEAST TWO YEARS OR BE A FREELANCER TO TRANSFER SUB-STUDIOS.

A BRAND NEW INBETWEENER PERSONALLY ASKING A DIRECTOR TO DO SOMETHING LIKE THAT IS EXTREMELY INAPPROPRIATE.
BUT...!

MS. DATE.

WE'RE GOING BACK TO STUDIO 2.

BOW
I'M VERY SORRY FOR DISTURBING YOU.

ANYWAY, COME BACK WHEN YOU MAKE KEY ANIMATOR.

...
WILL YOU TAKE ME INSTEAD OF MIYUKI IF I DO?

IF YOU CAN PRODUCE EXCELLENT WORK, I DON'T CARE WHO YOU ARE.

THINGS ARE STARTING TO GET INTERESTING...

PEOPLE HAVE EXTREMELY HIGH EXPECTATIONS FOR N2'S FILM PRODUCTIONS.
MAYBE GOOD STAFF AREN'T AVAILABLE, MAYBE THE SCHEDULE AND BUDGET ARE EXTREMELY TIGHT,
BUT NONE OF THAT MATTERS TO THE AUDIENCE.
IF THE FILM TURNS OUT POORLY, THE DIRECTOR SHOULDERS ALL THE BLAME.
AND WHAT HAPPENS NEXT? WELL, THAT DIRECTOR WILL HAVE A HARDER TIME FINDING MONEY AND STAFF FOR THEIR NEXT PROJECT.
OR, WORST CASE, THERE MIGHT NOT EVEN ***BE*** A NEXT PROJECT.

A DEAD PRODUCTION MEANS A DEAD DIRECTOR,
WHICH IS WHY DIRECTORS ALWAYS HAVE TO MAKE THE OPTIMAL CHOICES TO PRODUCE A GOOD END PRODUCT.

BUT THAT'S ALSO WHY DIRECTOR KUJO PUTS HIS LIFE ON THE LINE TO MAKE HIS WORK.
THE RESPONSIBILITY HE BEARS IS ON A COMPLETELY DIFFERENT LEVEL FROM OURS.

IF YOU HAVE IDEAS ABOUT HOW TO IMPROVE A PROJECT, THEN BY ALL MEANS SPEAK UP.
BUT IF YOU'RE JUST THINKING ABOUT YOURSELF, DO NOT QUESTION A DIRECTOR'S DECISIONS.
THAT IS ONE OF THE UNSPOKEN RULES OF THIS INDUSTRY.

YES, SIR...
BUT YOU CAN ALWAYS TALK TO ME IF YOU HAVE ANY ISSUES, SO DON'T HESITATE.
STUDIO 2
I GUESS EVERYONE WENT TO STUDIO 7...
Slurp
Slurp
KTCHK!
I'M BACK.
UM, WHAT HAPPENED WITH MARIA?
...YOU DON'T HAVE THE TIME TO BE SITTING HERE, SLURPING NOODLES LIKE AN IDIOT.
HUH...?

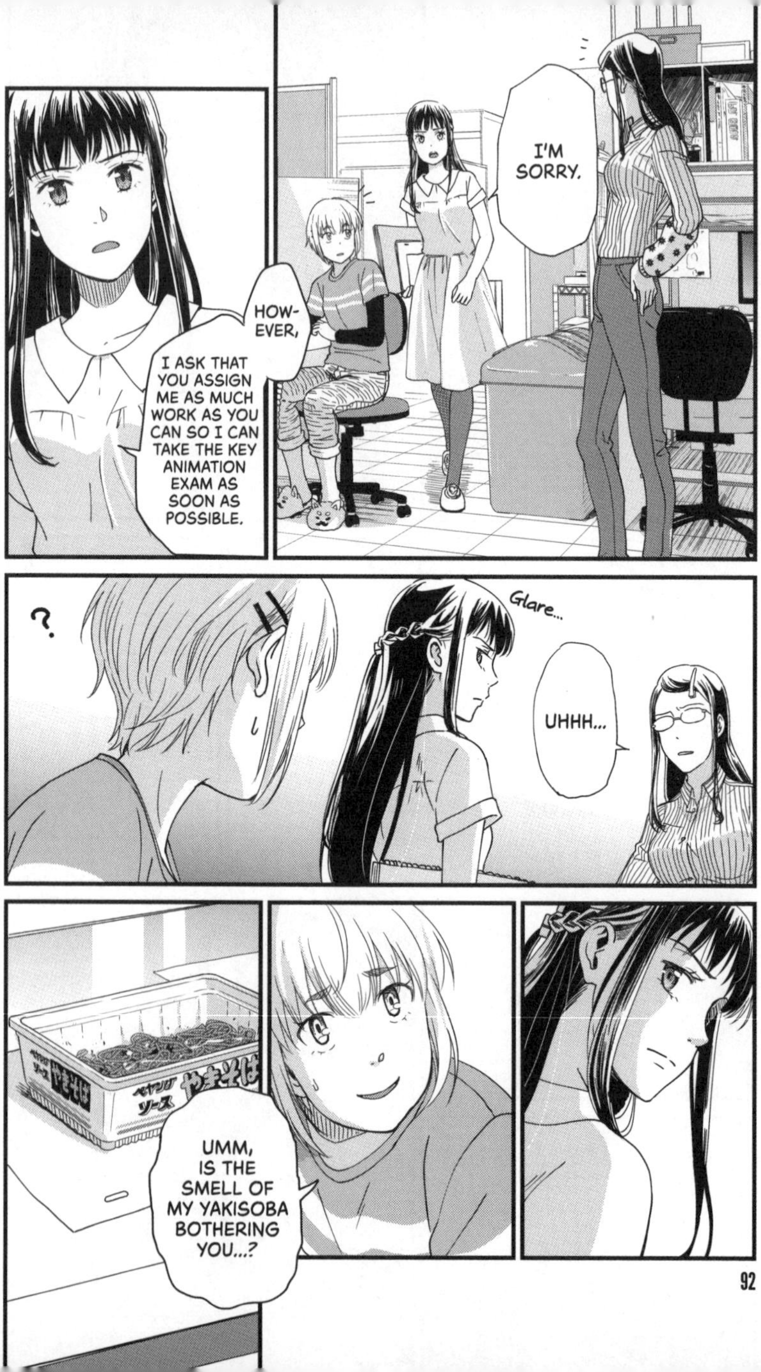

I'M SORRY.

HOW-EVER,

I ASK THAT YOU ASSIGN ME AS MUCH WORK AS YOU CAN SO I CAN TAKE THE KEY ANIMATION EXAM AS SOON AS POSSIBLE.

...
GUESS THAT WASN'T IT...
ガタ
SHNK!

Sketch
Sketch
Sketch
パラ
FLIP
パラ
FLIP

THREE DAYS LATER...
STUDIO
GOOD MORNING!
MOR—
OH, IT'S JUST YOU.

THAT REMINDS ME THOUGH, I HEARD A RUMOR YESTERDAY. IS IT TRUE?
WHAT?
I HEARD THAT WHEN MARIA MAKES KEY ANIMATOR, STUDIO 7 IS GONNA GIVE YOU THE AXE.

HUH?
WHO TOLD YOU THAT?

WELL, AT THE RATE YOU'RE GOING, YOU WON'T BE READY TO TAKE THE EXAM IN A YEAR ANYWAY.
YOU'RE GETTING FIRED, NO MATTER WHAT.

...

EXCUSE ME.

I'M FINISHED.
PLEASE GIVE ME MY NEXT CUT.
OH, GOOD.
PUT IT ON THE COMPLETED SHELF.

IT'S SATURDAY, AND PRETTY LATE AS IT IS.

I'LL HAVE SOMETHING FOR YOU ON MONDAY, SO WHY DON'T YOU JUST HEAD HOME?

I WAS PLANNING TO WORK ON SUNDAY AS WELL, SO PLEASE GIVE ME SOMETHING NOW. I DON'T MIND IF IT'S DIFFICULT.

CLATTER!
NIGHT!
GOOD NIGHT.

ALRIGHT THEN, HERE'S YOUR NEXT CUT.

AND AS FOR YOU, YUKIMURA, REDO THIS.

OOF...
D6 END

N2 FACTORY STUDIO
MAN, THAT MARIA CHICK SURE LOVES TO SHOW OFF.
ME ON THE OTHER HAND, I'D RATHER STICK TO EASY CUTS TO MAKE IT TO KEY ANIMATOR ASAP.

for you to get off work~
I'm done ＼(＾O＾)／
Read
23:18
GJ, dude (´Д`)/ I'm out having drinks with some people from TAIGA Anime, you in? There's this real cute production assistant chick here lmao
23:20
HELL YEAH! I'M TOTALLY IN ♡
SEND

WAS THAT FOUR-EYED JERK TELLING THE TRUTH...?
I'M IN REAL TROUBLE IF IT'S TRUE...
I ♥ 48
I KNEW IT! WE WERE WATCHING TV BACK IN OUR ROOM EARLIER,
AND WE SAW YOUR NAME IN THE END CREDITS!
INBETWEEN CHECKER
TOMOMI SHINOZAKI
INBETWEENS
TAEKO OOBAYASHI
NOZOMU HARIMAYA
MIZUKI SONOMIYA
KOUTA KASAGI
MARIA DATE

Total Frames for 4/1 - 4/30

Azuma	492
Makimura	380

0

256

Fuji

Totsuka

Sanada

Date

Natou

SO, YOU'RE SAYING...
IF I WERE ATTACHED TO STUDIO 7, THERE WOULDN'T BE AN ISSUE?
CROQ
47...
Mmph...
BR
Twitch!
ビクッ
シャカ
Shk
シャカ
Shk
シャカ
Shk
シャカ
Shk
I ♥ 48

TV: Do Marimo Count as Pets?

Animation Exam Within A Year
500 frames in one month
CUT 315.
CUT 315.
CUT 315.
Key Animation Exam Within A Year
500 frames in one month
CUT 315.

CUT...
315!
SHARK

THAT MOMENT...
nepio

MARIMO'S LEG BRIEFLY CROSSED THE SCREEN...

AND IT ALL HAPPENED IN A TWELVE FRAME CUT THAT DIDN'T EVEN MAKE UP A FULL SECOND OF RUNTIME...

IT WAS A MERE
HALF SECOND

OF PRETTY
MUCH NOTHING

BUT IN THAT
MOMENT, I FELT
LIKE I WAS THE
ONLY PERSON
IN THE ENTIRE
WORLD.

OH...

I ONLY WORKED ON ONE CUT, SO MY NAME ISN'T IN THE CREDITS.

MS. FUJI HAD TO CORRECT IT A BUNCH, TOO...

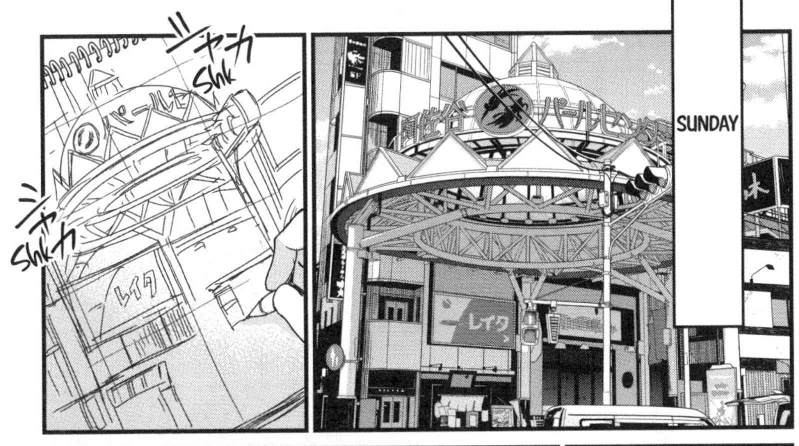
SUNDAY
シャカ
Shk
シャカ
Shk

I TRIED DRAWING EVERYTHING I SAW,
BUT THIS IS ALL I MANAGED IN ONE DAY.

HM, EVERYTHING I CAN SEE...
IT'S GETTING DARK OUT.
MAYBE I'LL SWING BY THE STUDIO TO GET A LITTLE WORK DONE BEFORE GOING HOME.

STUDIO 2
ガチャ
KTCHK

OH... GOOD EVENING.
パラ
Flip
パラ
Flip
...GOOD EVENING.

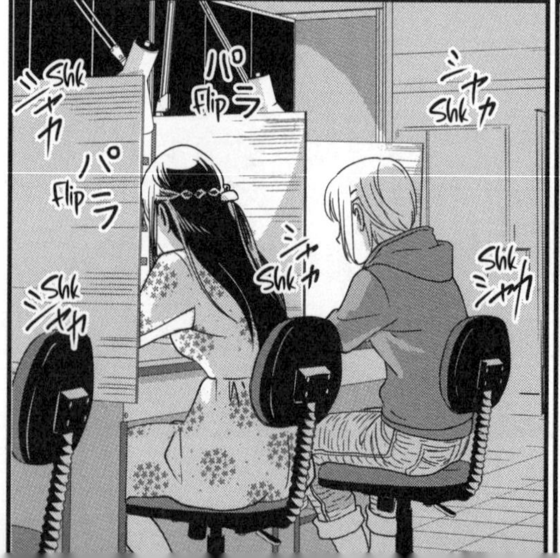
シャカ
Shk
パラ
Flip
シャカ
Shk
パラ
Flip
シャカ
Shk
シャカ
Shk
シャカ
Shk

MONDAY
N2 FACTORY STUDIO
CHORE WHEEL
TRASH
Yukimura
Sanada
Date
Natou
OFF
KITCH
ONCE A WEEK, TURN THE WHEEL
HEHE HEH...
I'VE BEEN LOOKING FORWARD TO THIS DAY FOR TWO WHOLE WEEKS!
This is what I call happiness!
IT'S AN ALL-I-CAN-PICK BUFFET!
I'M DINING ON ROUGH FRAMES TONIGHT!
MISTRESS KYOUKO♡ USE YOUR STILETTOS PLEASEEE...
HE HAS MORE THAN ONE?
すぴょー
SNOOORE!
IT'S HARD TO BELIEVE THE PERSON ALWAYS SLEEPING ON THE FLOOR HERE IS A GODLY ANIMATOR...

...

Rustle...

SPELLBOUND...

OH MY GOD, WHAT A CATCH! WHAT A CATCH!

I WISH I WAS ON GARBAGE DUTY EVERY WEEK...

THE NEXT DAY

THIS ONE'S MR. IGARASHI'S.
AND THIS IS... PROBABLY MR. ASAISHI'S.
HIS LINES ARE A LOT MESSIER THAN I WOULD'VE THOUGHT.
ガサ RUSTLE
ガサ RUSTLE
ガサ RUSTLE
ガサ RUSTLE
ガサ RUSTLE
ガサ RUSTLE

バッ
TAP
パラ
FLIP
パラ
FLIP
パラ
FLIP
CROQUIS
SHIBA
WAIT, IS THIS...?

Haaa...
BATHS ARE THE LAUNDRY OF THE SOUL...
CHAPTER 14: INBETWEEN CHECKER – PART A
SPLASH!
I BETTER GET OUT NOW OR I'LL MISS IT.

WHY ARE YOU CALLING SO LATE?

YOU NEVER PICK UP AT ANY OTHER TIME, SO IT'S NOT LIKE I HAVE MUCH CHOICE.

YEAH, BECAUSE I HAVE A JOB AND I NEED TO SLEEP. I LITERALLY JUST GOT HOME.

MOM

Speaker

Keypad

Contacts

FaceTime

Add Call

COME HOME AND GET MARRIED SO YOU CAN PUT YOUR POOR MOTHER'S MIND AT EASE!
YOU'RE THE ONLY ONE OF MY GIRLS WHO ISN'T MARRIED YET, HONEY!
THE MAN I PICKED OUT EVEN LIKES ANIME AND DOESN'T MIND IF YOU KEEP WORKING.
AT LEAST MEET HIM AND SEE WHAT YOU THINK!
YOU'RE TURNING 30 THIS YEAR. YOU WON'T BE YOUNG FOREVER.
OR WHAT, HAVE YOU ALREADY MET SOMEONE YOU LIKE?

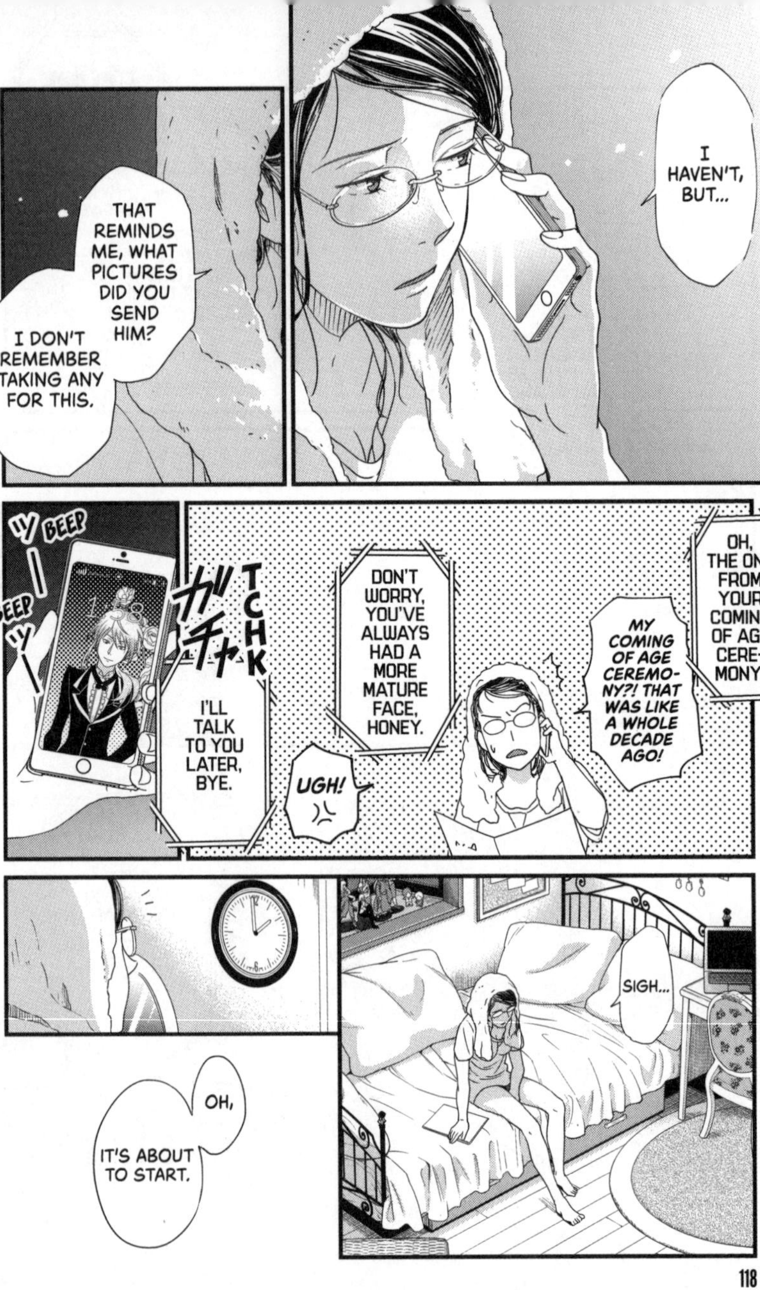

I HAVEN'T, BUT...
THAT REMINDS ME, WHAT PICTURES DID YOU SEND HIM?
I DON'T REMEMBER TAKING ANY FOR THIS.

TV: Do Marimo Count As Pets?
マリモはペットにはいりますか？

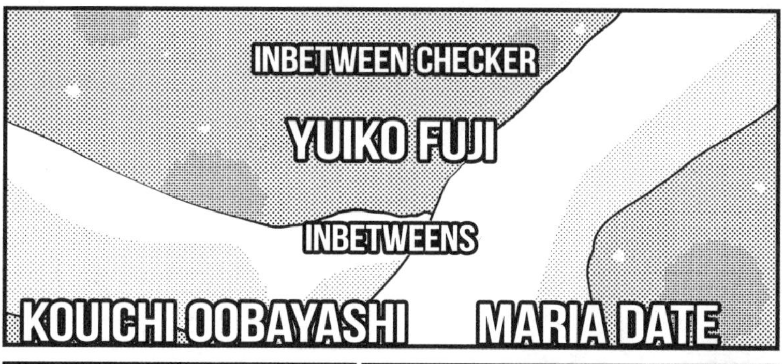
INBETWEEN CHECKER
YUIKO FUJI
INBETWEENS
KOUICHI OOBAYASHI
MARIA DATE

Peel
Peel

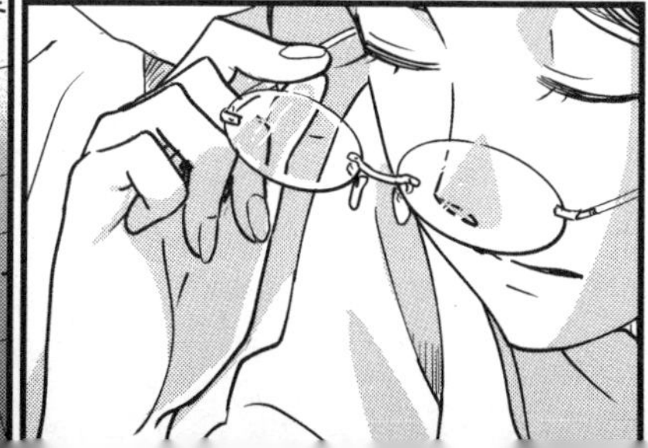

92%
SoftBonk 3G
Cancel
MariPet
MariPet
Search for images for MariPet
公式マリモはペットにはいりま
@marimohapetto
ブスマリペ民
fakieks12
あ
か
な

AD (Sakkan): Short for Animation Director (sakuga kantoku).
The AD's job is to correct keyframes to ensure uniformity in the art of a production.

Botamochi@
Damn, that was amazing...
The person who animated that cut at the lake is a god. It was so fucking good.

I love rice so much I can't stand it@goha... 1m
God-tier episode of MariPet!!!!!!

Shinmei@6/15 Pilgrimage to Lake Akan 1m
The action in that ep of MariPet must've been Tama-chan, right? It was sooo cool! Thank you based Tama-chan!!

Izanami@on a diet (currently 130lbs)
Wow, the animation in this episode of MariPet was gorgeous! They're really putting their all in this. The AD, Souji Igarashi, always produced film-grade wo

EVEN WHEN AN EPISODE GETS PRAISED FOR HAVING GOD-TIER ANIMATION, THE DIRECTORS AND KEY ANIMATORS GET ALL THE CREDIT.

NO ONE CARES HOW MUCH WORK WENT INTO CLEANING UP THEIR MESSES.

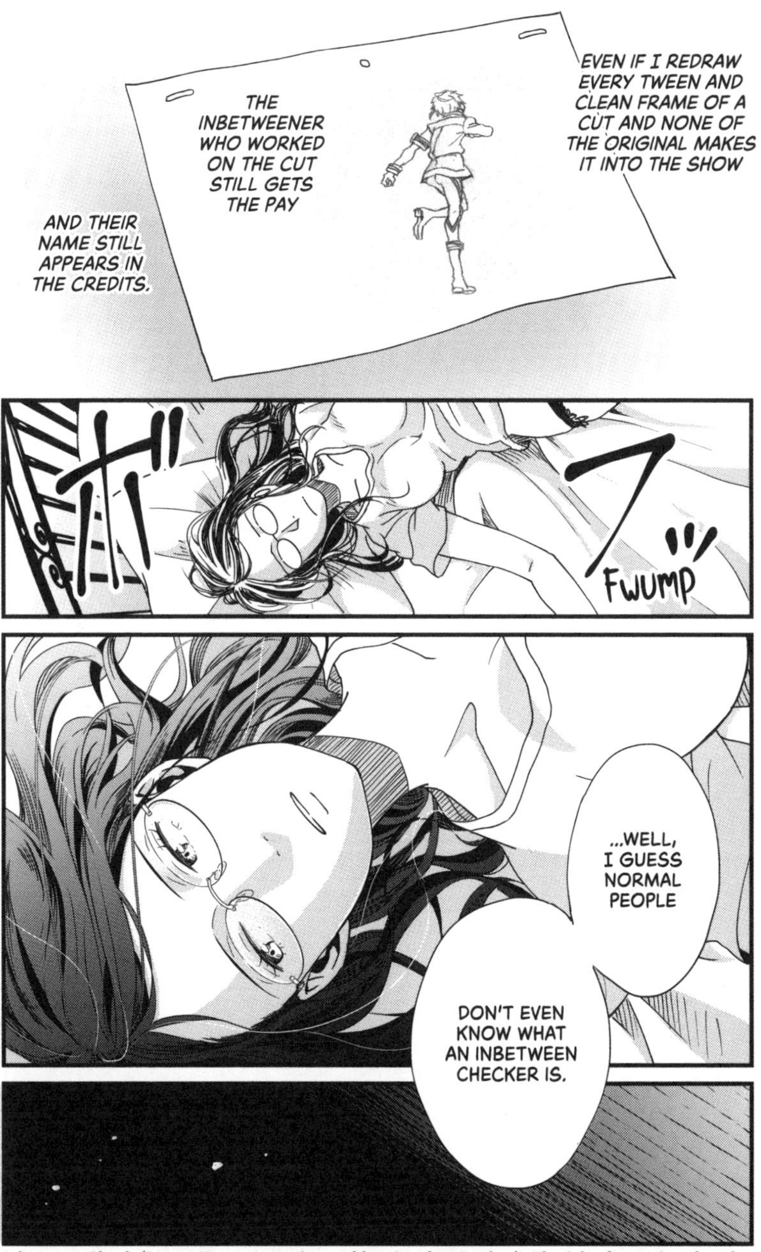

Inbetween Check (Douga Kensa, sometimes abbreviated to Douken): The job of ensuring that the inbetweens are neat and the motion smooth. Similar to the job of the Animation Director (sakuga kantoku) but for inbetweens and cleanup rather than key animation.

MONDAY

STUDIO 7

I FINISHED MY SECOND SKETCHBOOK, SO PLEASE TAKE A LOOK.

CROQUIS

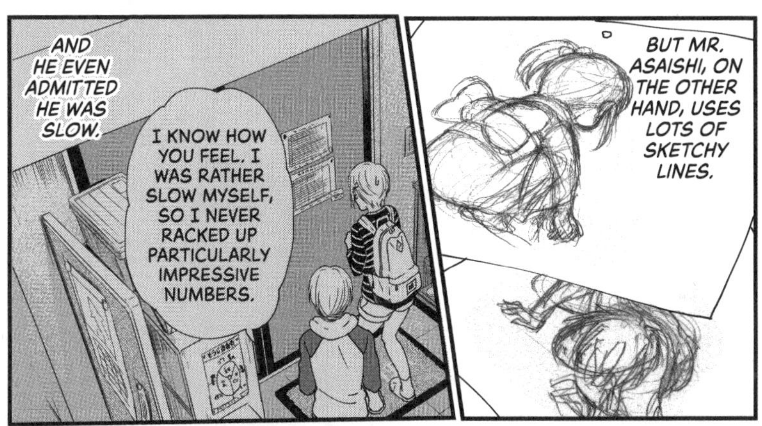
AND HE EVEN ADMITTED HE WAS SLOW.
I KNOW HOW YOU FEEL. I WAS RATHER SLOW MYSELF, SO I NEVER RACKED UP PARTICULARLY IMPRESSIVE NUMBERS.
BUT MR. ASAISHI, ON THE OTHER HAND, USES LOTS OF SKETCHY LINES.

I'M NOT VERY GOOD AT DRAWING, SO I DON'T KNOW WHAT'S "RIGHT." I JUST KEEP HESITATING AND PUTTING DOWN MORE LINES RATHER THAN MAKING CONFIDENT MARKS.
MY WORK HAS SO MANY UNNECESSARY LINES. THAT'S WHY IT TAKES ME SO LONG.

SO, BASICALLY, TO GET FASTER,
I NEED TO LEARN TO USE FEWER, MORE CONFIDENT LINES IN MY WORK.

YOU STILL SUCK.
THAT SAID, YOUR DECISION TO DO YOUR BEST TO REDUCE THE NUMBER OF LINES YOU'RE USING WAS CORRECT.
YOU'D HAVE NO CHANCE OF IMPROVING IF YOU KEEP PRODUCING WORK WITH ALL THOSE POINTLESS LINES.
I WAS RIGHT!
THANK YOU SO MUCH!

WELL, I HAVE CLEANING DUTIES TO ATTEND TO, SO I'LL BE HEADING BACK TO STUDIO 2 NOW!
Uuugh!
SHE SURE IS CHIPPER FIRST THING IN THE MORNING...
ムクリ
SHMP
FLIP FLIP
FLIP FLIP
WOW, DID SHE REALLY BRING YOU ANOTHER FILLED OUT SKETCHBOOK ALREADY?
HUH, SHE'S ACTUALLY GOTTEN A LITTLE BETTER.

OH! GOOD MORNING!

MORN-ING.

EPISODE 6 OF MARIPET WAS SO WELL ANIMATED!
I WANT TO BE ABLE TO DRAW KEY ANIMATION LIKE THAT SOON!
WELL, WHY NOT START BY MAKING YOUR WAY TO DRAWING 500 FRAMES A MONTH.
Rustle
YES, MA'AM! I'LL DO MY BEST!
...THEN HURRY UP AND GET BACK TO YOUR DESK.
OKAY!

TWO WEEKS LATER
SHHHHH
YUKIMURA, THIS IS YOUR NEXT CUT.
OH!
WHAT?
OH, IT'S JUST, THIS IS MY FIRST PROPER CHARACTER CUT.
I'M SO HAPPY!
Ehehe

YES...

パラ FLIP
パラ FLIP
パラパラ FLIP
パラ FLIP
パラ FLIP

パラ FLIP
パラ FLIP
パラ FLIP

SHE CHECKS THE MOTION SO CAREFULLY...

パラ FLIP
パラ FLIP
パラ FLIP

HUH?
OH... OKAY.
SHE GOT IT DONE A LOT FASTER THAN I EXPECTED.
YOU STARTING TO GET THE HANG OF IT?
I AM!
AT FIRST, WHEN I WAS DOING CLEANUP, I WAS JUST LOOKING AT A SINGLE KEYFRAME
AND I REALLY STRUGGLED WITH STRAY LINES AND LINES THAT DIDN'T CONNECT.
BUT WHEN I FLIPPED THROUGH THE KEYFRAMES SEVERAL TIMES BEFORE I STARTED CLEANUP, AND GOT A FEEL FOR THE FULL MOTION,
IT GOT SO MUCH EASIER TO TELL WHICH LINES WERE IMPORTANT AND WHICH ONES WEREN'T.

Cleanup: Tracing and applying corrections to raw keyframes (genga).

UM...
HAVE YOU TAKEN THE KEY ANIMATION EXAM, MS. FUJI?

WELL... THAT'S A GOOD QUES-TION.
IT WAS SO LONG AGO THAT I'VE LONG SINCE FORGOTTEN ABOUT IT.

TAP TAP
HERE. REDO THIS.

I'M HEADING HOME, SO DROP IT ON THE COMPLETED SHELF ONCE YOU'RE DONE FIXING IT UP.
HUH...?
ARE YOU SURE YOU DON'T NEED TO CHECK IT AGAIN?
IT'LL BE FINE.
...I'M SO HAPPY!
YOU SHOULDN'T BE SO HAPPY ABOUT HAVING TO REDO A CUT.

BUT...
I FEEL LIKE YOU'RE STARTING TO TRUST ME JUST A LITTLE,
WHICH MAKES ME HAPPY!
YEAH, I USED TO BE JUST LIKE HER.
FUJI, YOU PASS PROVISIONALLY.

Second Key Animation (Nigen): The job involves taking the rough motion of the first key animation (layout) and cleaning it up and polishing it to create a completed key animation sequence.

HER KEY ANIMATION IS BORING.
OH, YOU'RE TALKING ABOUT FUJI'S WORK...

YEAH, I KNOW WHAT YOU'RE SAYING. SHE WORKS HARD, BUT NOTHING SHE PRODUCES IS INTERESTING, THOUGH IT'S NOT LIKE IT'S UNUSABLE OR ANYTHING.

GUESS IT'S TRUE WHAT THEY SAY.
BEING GOOD AT INBETWEENING DOESN'T MEAN YOU'LL BE A GOOD KEY ANIMATOR.

I'M REALLY SORRY TO BOTHER YOU WITH THIS, SINCE I KNOW YOU'RE DOING KEY ANIMATION ALREADY,
Royal Girl Panna
BUT WOULD YOU PLEASE TWEEN AND CLEAN THIS CUT...

OH, IT'S FINE... I'M A LOT BETTER AT TWEENING ANYWAY...
YOU'RE A REAL LIFESAVER!

STUDIO 2

COULD YOU POINT ME TO THE DESK OF AN INBETWEENER NAMED FUJI?

THERE AREN'T MANY PEOPLE WHO CAN DRAW TWEENS SO FAITHFUL TO THE ORIGINAL KEY ANIMATION.
YOU'RE TOP CLASS, NOT JUST IN OUR STUDIO, BUT THE ENTIRE INDUSTRY.
TO ME... THOSE WORDS...

...WERE A CRUEL...
...KIND-NESS...
SO, WHY DON'T YOU JOIN STUDIO 7 AS OUR INBETWEEN CHECKER?
Title
Royal Girl Pannacotta
MEMO/CAMERA
Horizontal Pan
*Please give this to an in-house inbetweener!
N2 FACTORY STUDI

WELL,
I HAVE A DATE WITH A HOT GUY, SO I NEED TO GET GOING.
YOU HAVE A BOY-FRIEND?!
THAT'S WHAT I SAID.
WHAT'S HE LIKE?!

ガチャッ
KTCHK
HE'S A BARD WITH LONG BLOND HAIR AND A KNIGHTSHIP.
WH... WHOA...

OH, OFF FOR THE NIGHT?
...
WHAT?
NOTH-ING...
HERE TO STEAL MORE SNACKS?

Fully Corrected (Zenshu): When someone in a supervisory role (animation director, inbetween checker, etc) redraws work from scratch instead of correcting portions of individual frames.

YOU'RE AMAZING, FUJIKO.

AND HE KEEPS DOING IT.

OH! DIRECTOR KUJO!

DO YOU MIND TAKING A LOOK AT THIS FOR ME?

YOU SURE IT'S NOT GOING TO TURN OUT LIKE LAST TIME?

IT'LL BE FINE!
PROB-ABLY!

コッ
TAP
TAP
コッ
ガチャ
KTCHK
コッ
TAP
コッ
TAP
コッ
TAP
ザアアアア
SHHHHHH
N2 FACTORY STU O
MR. KUJO'S WORDS CON- TINUE TO BIND ME.
IT'S JUST NOT FAIR...

ヴ BUZZ
ヴ BUZZ
ヴ BUZZ
ヴ
MOM
BUZZ ヴ
BUZZ ヴ
BUZZ ヴ
ヴ
BUZZ ヴ
BUZZ ヴ
BUZZ ヴ
MAYBE I'M THE ONE BEING UNFAIR.

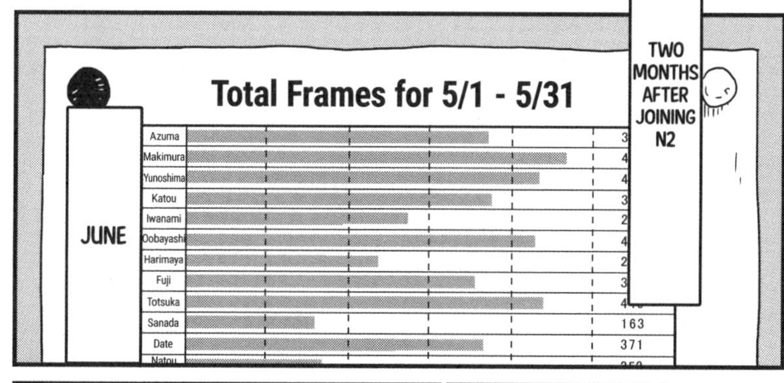
TWO MONTHS AFTER JOINING N2
Total Frames for 5/1 - 5/31
JUNE
Azuma
Makimura
Yunoshima
Katou
Iwanami
Oobayashi
Harimaya
Fuji
Totsuka
Sanada
163
Date
371

...163 FRAMES.

IF I CAN'T GET BETTER QUICKLY,
I JUST HAVE TO DO WHAT I CAN.

FIRST, I NEED TO FOCUS ON GETTING FASTER AT CLEANUP.
Shk
Shk
Shk

THREE MONTHS AFTER JOINING N2

Total Frames for 6/1 - 6/30

461
380
371
375
256
487

JULY

230 FRAMES ...

REDO IT.

Flip
Flip
Flip
Flip
Flip
Flip
Flip
Flip
Shk
Shk
Shk
Shk
Shk
Shk

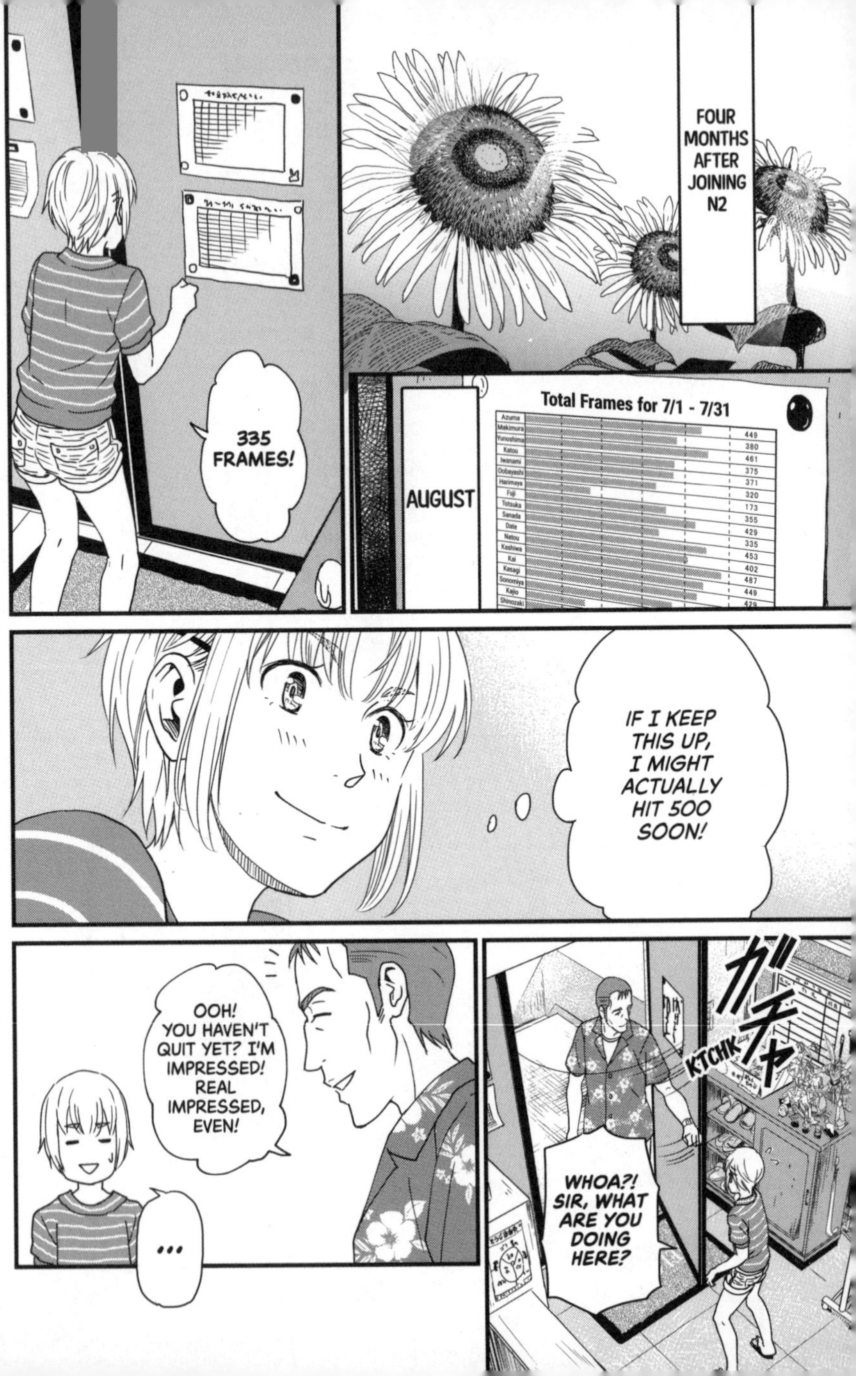

FOUR MONTHS AFTER JOINING N2

AUGUST

Total Frames for 7/1 - 7/31

Name	Frames
Azuma	449
Makimura	380
Yunoshima	461
Katou	375
Iwanami	371
Oobayashi	320
Harimaya	173
Fuji	355
Totsuka	429
Sanada	335
Date	453
Natou	402
Kashiwa	487
Kai	449
Kasagi	429
Sonomiya	
Kajio	
Shinozaki	

335 FRAMES!

BY THE WAY, IS OUR LITTLE MARIA HERE?

LITTLE MARIA?

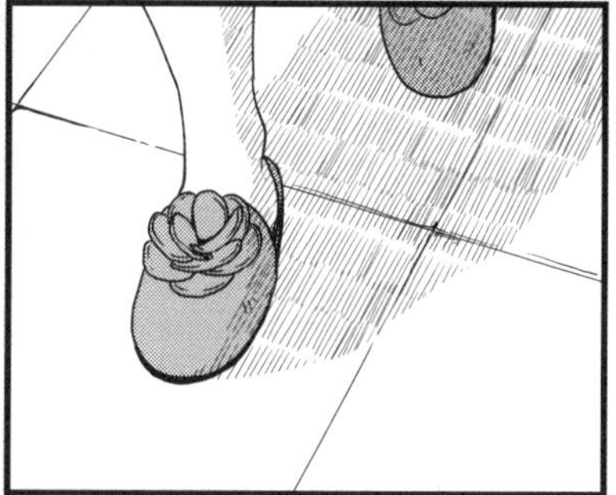

OOH, LITTLE MARIA!

...
WHAT?

OH, NOTHING IN PARTICULAR.

BABY!
WANNA TRY YOUR HAND AT CHARACTER DESIGN?
HUH?! CHARACTER DESIGN?!

Bonus Follow Through in Tweening

Fluttering follow through

Hair on B①

Face and body paused on A①

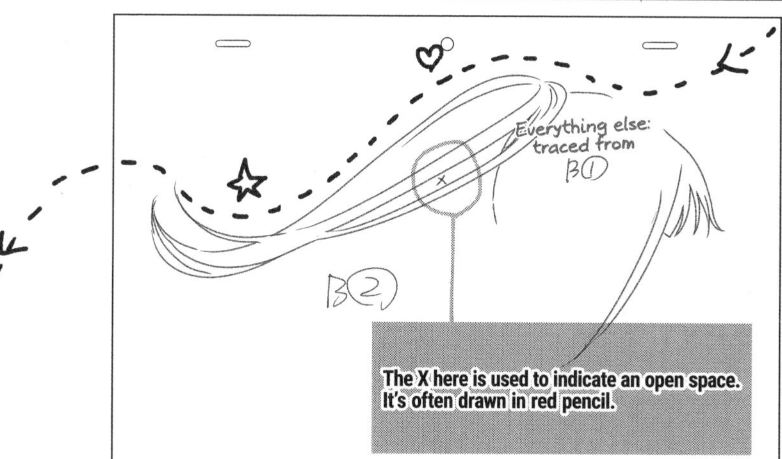

• In the above example, there's an invisible line moving from right to left indicating the "wave form" of the wind. Think of the ♡ mark as following a peak as it moves from B① to B②, and the ☆ as following a valley as it moves between the two key frames.

• We call this kind of tweening "follow through."

• Parts of frames are designated to be traced off previous keyframes when the animator doesn't want those still parts of the image to look perfectly frozen. In the above example, in B② there's a note to trace the remaining section of the head off frame B①.

Everything copied from A①

Coming up from out of frame

Repeat

- In this example, the inbetweener is asked to create a loop using just frame A①. The contents of A① are copied completely to create A② and then tweened with follow through from the bottom left to upper right just like on the previous page.
- When there is no timing chart provided to create a follow through loop like this, tweens will be evenly spaced.
- Another example of a tweened follow through loop is the part in Sailor Moon's transformation sequence where her skirt twirls.
- By the way, cuts that make up sequences that are used over and over again, like transformation sequences for example, are called "bank" or stock footage.

FOLLOW THROUGH IS A MUST WHEN TWEENING THINGS LIKE WIND, FIRE, CLOTH, HAIR, SMOKE, WATER, LIGHT, AND MANY OTHER THINGS.

USING FOLLOW THROUGH TO CREATE A SKIRT TWIRL PROBABLY WON'T PRODUCE THE MOST REALISTIC VISUALS, BUT THAT'S PART OF WHAT MAKES ANIMATION SO INTERESTING: THERE ARE SO MANY DIFFERENT APPROACHES TO SIMILAR SUBJECT MATTER!

LEVEL UP!
♪ Do-do-do-do-doo-doo-do-do-do~ ♪
Original Concept
Character Designer
Chief Animation Director
Animation Director
Key Animator
Inbetween Checker
Inbetweener
Yukimura's mental image of the hierarchy of animators

JUMPING STRAIGHT FROM INBETWEENS TO CHARACTER DESIGN...
ISN'T THAT LIKE A PEASANT SUDDENLY BEING OFFERED A LORDSHIP?!

CHAPTER 15: YUKIMURA'S SUMMER VACATION

IT'S NOT GONNA BE EASY,
BUT I JUST THOUGHT...
I'LL DO IT!

ガチャ
KTCHK
GREAT. I'LL BRING YOU SOME REFERENCE MATERIALS LATER.
YES, SIR!

OH!

JUST WHO I WAS LOOKIN' FOR!
TAKE THIS TO STUDIO 7 FOR ME, WOULD YA?
TLE
RUS
WHAT IS IT?
PORTFOLIOS OF THE PEOPLE WHO TOOK THE ENTRANCE EXAM THIS YEAR.

...
STUDIO 7... DID THEY PASS ANYONE?
SURE DID.
THESE ARE THE BEST, MOST POPULAR CANDIDATES.

C-CAN I TAKE A PEEK?
GO RIGHT AHEAD.

RUSTLE
RUSTLE
RUSTLE
RUSTLE

...
THEY'RE ALL AMAZING.

HOW DID I PASS THE FIRST ROUND?
OH,
I PASSED YOU 'CAUSE YOU PUT DOWN THAT YOU HAD A SECOND DEGREE BLACK BELT IN JUDO.
...What?
That's why I passed?!
MAYBE LUCK'S ALL YOU'VE REALLY GOT.
WITH HOW BAD YOUR ART WAS, YOU SHOULD'VE GOTTEN THE AXE IN THE SECOND ROUND,
BUT KUJO PUSHED FOR YOU HARD, SO YOU GOT THROUGH.
WE'LL TALK LATER, THEN...
UNDER-STOOD.
2 FACTORY STUDIO

STILL, NEXT YEAR'S BATCH OF NEW HIRES ARE PRETTY GOOD.
Sigh...
Not A Winner
STUDIO 7 MIGHT NOT NEED YOU IF YOU CAN'T KEEP UP.
LISTEN UP,
THIS IS A WORLD WHERE WORDS LIKE "ABILITY" AND "TALENT" MEAN EVERYTHING.

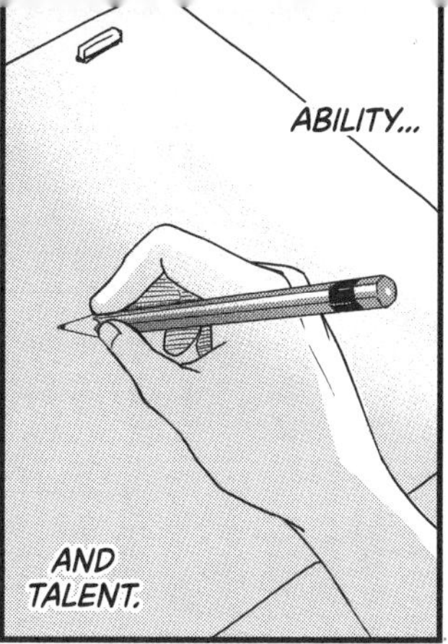
ABILITY...
AND TALENT.

I DON'T THINK I HAVE EITHER OF THOSE...
YUKI-MURA.

YES?

YOU'RE TAKING YOUR SUMMER VACATION AT THE END OF AUGUST.
WHAT?!

I WAS GOING TO SKIP IT AND WORK THE WHOLE TIME...

BZZT! INCOR-RECT!

PEOPLE DIE IF THEY DON'T TAKE BREAKS.
SO WHAT DO YOU SAY WHEN YOUR SUPERIOR TELLS YOU, A NEWBIE, TO TAKE YOUR VACATION?
...YES, MA'AM.

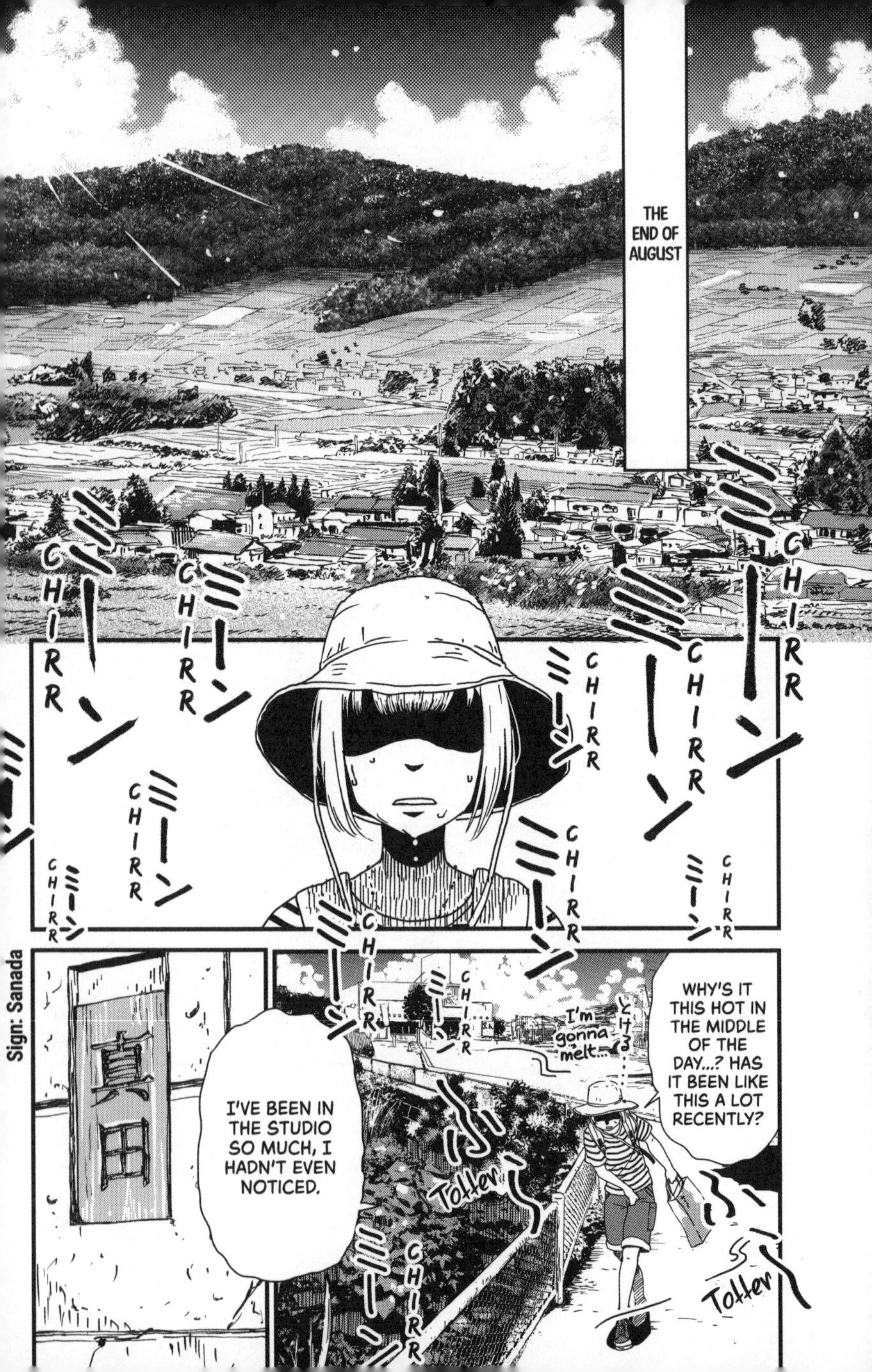

THE END OF AUGUST
CHIRR
CHIRR
CHIRR
CHIRR
CHIRR
CHIRR
CHIRR
CHIRR
CHIRR
WHY'S IT THIS HOT IN THE MIDDLE OF THE DAY...? HAS IT BEEN LIKE THIS A LOT RECENTLY?
I'm gonna melt...
とける…
Totter
Totter
CHIRR
CHIRR
I'VE BEEN IN THE STUDIO SO MUCH, I HADN'T EVEN NOTICED.
CHIRR
真田
Sign: Sanada

CHIRR
CHIRR
I'M FINALLY HOME...
CHIRR
CHIRR

I'M BACK!
Shhk
TNK
TNK
TNK
JUMP

キュキュウーン
WOOF!
MANSASHI!
パタ
Step
パタ
Step
モフ モフ
SQUISH SQUISH
RUB
スリ
スリ
RUB
HOW HAVE YOU BEEN, MANSASHI!
HUFF, I CAN'T GET ENOUGH OF YOUR DOG SMELL!
MIYU-KI?!
WHAT ARE YOU DOING HOME? DID YOU QUIT?
NO, IT'S JUST SUMMER VACATION.
HOW LONG WILL YOU BE HERE?
DO YOU WANT DINNER?
AND WHY ARE YOU DRESSED LIKE THAT?
WOULD IT KILL YOU TO WEAR A SKIRT?
RUSTLE
ごそ
RUSTLE
ごそ

HEY! GIVE ME MY WALLET BACK!

FWIP

Pant

Pant

GLARE...
SO, YOU STILL HAVE A THING FOR 10,000 YEN NOTES, HUH?
ギン
ハッ Pant
ハッ Pant
ハッ Pant
ハッ Pant
IF ONLY YOU'D FIND ME TWO HUNDRED MILLION IN A BAMBOO GROVE SOME-WHERE...

...

ALRIGHT! MANSASHI, LET'S GO FOR A WALK!
キューン WHINE
プリ Wag
プリ Wag

スン Sniff
スン Sniff

WHAT? YOU FIND SOME-THING?
WOOF!
Dig ホリ
ホリ Dig
ホリ Dig
ホリ Dig
A K-KOKESHI DOLL?! ...THAT'S KINDA CREEPY, SO LET'S PUT IT BACK...
Ah...
カナ Shirr
カナ Shirr
カナ Shirr
カナ Shirr
カナ Shirr
カナ Shirr
カナ Shirr
カナ Shirr
カナ Shirr
THE CICADAS...

Ahh...

OKAY, LET'S HEAD HOME!
Dinner time!
WOOF!

HUH?
IS THAT YOU, MIYUKIN?!

I HAVEN'T SEEN YOU SINCE GRADUATION!
You haven't changed at all!
Oh...
Oh, Mansashi!
HEY GUYS, IT'S BEEN AGES!

YOU'RE WORKING IN TOKYO NOW, RIGHT?
SURE AM. I'M BACK FOR SUMMER VACATION.

I HEAR YOU'RE AN ANIMATOR NOW.
UM, YEAH...
OH, RIGHT, YOU WERE ALWAYS INTO THAT STUFF, WEREN'T YOU?
YOU MADE YOUR DREAM COME TRUE, HUH?
THAT'S AMAZING!
Total Frames for 6/1 - 6/30
461
380
371
375
256
487
IT'S REALLY NOTHING SPECIAL.

SERIOUSLY? THE PAY MUST BE PRETTY GOOD AT LEAST.
I MEAN, IT'S IN TOKYO AND IT'S THE ENTERTAINMENT INDUSTRY.
NO... THE PAY IS... REALLY BAD...
WELL, I'M STILL JEALOUS. YOU HAVE YOUR DREAM JOB.
YEAH, SERIOUSLY. WE'RE JUST WORKING PART-TIME AT THE POST OFFICE RIGHT NOW.
OH, WHAT'S THAT NECKLACE?
A PRESENT FROM YOUR BOYFRIEND?!
TWITCH
NO... THAT'S NOT WHAT IT...
I WANNA SEE! I WANNA SEE!

WOW, IT'S A LOCKET EVEN!
LOOK...
IS THERE A PHOTO OF YOUR BOYFRIEND IN THERE?!
POP!
パカ

ISN'T HE A LITTLE OLD?
For you, I mean.
LIKE I SAID, HE'S NOT MY BOYFRIEND.
HIS NAME IS MR. SERIZAWA AND HE'S AN ANIME DIRECTOR I ADMIRE...
WHAT? HOLD UP,
YOU'RE TELLING ME YOU WALK AROUND WITH A PHOTO OF YOUR FAVORITE ANIME DIRECTOR IN A LOCKET?

THAT'S PRETTY... YIKES...
?
YIKES FOR SURE.

OH, LOOK AT THE TIME!
WE'RE GOING TO BE LATE FOR WORK.
TALK TO YOU LATER!
OH, UH... SURE, LATER.
Nirasaki

Better hurry!

LET'S GO HOME.

Whine
キュ

ーン

I'M BACK.

THERE'S SOMETHING SPECIAL ABOUT HAVING FOOD APPEAR ON THE TABLE WITHOUT HAVING TO DO ANYTHING YOURSELF...
It's melting in my mouth!

WHAT ARE YOU EATING OVER THERE?
I HOPE YOU'RE NOT TRYING TO SURVIVE ON INSTANT RAMEN.
UM...
WELL...

OH, YOU GOT A NEW TV...
AND A BLU-RAY RECORDER TOO...

I WANTED TO RECORD PANNACOTTA,
We only ever use the TV to watch the news anyway.
SO I'D BEG MOM EVERY SINGLE DAY, BUT SHE NEVER CAVED.
MOM! BUY ME A BLU-RAY RECORDER!
WE DON'T NEED IT. WE HAVE A VCR. ISN'T THAT GOOD ENOUGH?
BUT VHS IS SUCH LOW RESOLU-TION!

I CAUGHT A SPECIAL ON TV THE OTHER DAY.

IS IT TRUE THAT THEY MAKE YOU WORK LATE INTO THE NIGHT WITH NO BREAKS?

AND THEY MENTIONED MONTHLY WAGES UNDER 100,000 YEN. HOW CAN YOU EVEN CALL THAT A COMPANY?

YOU SHOULD QUIT NOW AND GO TO COLLEGE, OR TAKE THE CIVIL SERVICE EXAM AND LOOK FOR A GOVERNMENT JOB.

BOTH OF YOUR BROTHERS HAVE GOVERNMENT JOBS...
I'M TOO EMBARRASSED TO TELL ANYONE MY DAUGHTER'S AN ANIMATOR.

HEY, THIS IS THE FIRST TIME SHE'S BEEN HOME IN AGES. LAY OFF.
I MEAN, ANIME IS FOR CHILDREN AND EMOTIONALLY STUNTED WEIRDOS, ISN'T IT?
I WANT YOU TO QUIT FOOLING AROUND WITH CHILDISH NON-SENSE.
THE SOONER YOU GET A REAL JOB, THE BETTER.

CLATTER!
I DON'T KNOW A SINGLE PERSON IN THE INDUSTRY WHO'S "FOOLING AROUND"!

DON'T FORCE YOUR VALUES ON ME, MOM.
THINGS MIGHT BE ROUGH NOW,
BUT I'M HAPPY TO BE DOING WORK THAT I LOVE!

SHHK!
EXCUSE ME.
...WHERE DO YOU THINK YOU'RE GOING, MIYUKI?!
...
WHY DON'T WE JUST LET HER SEE THIS THROUGH?
YOU'VE ALWAYS BEEN TOO EASY ON HER.
I'M THINKING ABOUT HER HAPPINESS, YOU KNOW?
Sigh...
THAT'S FUNNY, CONSIDER-ING YOU BOUGHT THAT BLU-RAY MACHINE
AND RECORDED THE ANIME MIYUKI WORKED ON.

ONE WEEK LATER

N2 FACTORY STUDIO

HUH? STUDIO 7'S NEW HIRE QUIT?

I HAD HIGH HOPES TOO...

NOT MUCH WE CAN DO, UNFORTU-NATELY.

UM...
AM I BEING FIRED?
Kikyou Shingen Mochi
...
WOW, YOU LOOK LOVELY, MS. SANADA.
CLOTHES REALLY CAN WORK MIRACLES...
STARTLED

STUDIO CHAOS.

I'M SURE YOU KNOW,

BUT THAT'S SERIZAWA'S—PANNACOTTA'S DIRECTOR'S—NEW STUDIO.

I WONDER IF THIS HAS KUJO RATTLED.
I MEAN, OUR NEW HIRE GOT STOLEN BY SERIZAWA'S STUDIO OF ALL PLACES...
IS THERE SOME BAD BLOOD BETWEEN THEM?
KUJO AND SERIZAWA JOINED THE SAME YEAR, YOU SEE.
阿佐谷北1丁目
AND, WELL... IT'S COMPLICATED.

Crunch!
...SOLIN, SOLI'SA...
DJIP'TALOU...
DIRECTOR KUJO.
WHY ARE YOU...?
WHAT ARE YOU DOING HERE?

I COULD ASK YOU THE SAME QUESTION.
OH...
I, UH, COME HERE A LOT WHEN I NEED TO THINK.
NOT A LOT OF PEOPLE USE THIS CROSSING,
AND YOU CAN SEE WAY OFF INTO THE DISTANCE IF YOU LOOK STRAIGHT DOWN THE ROAD, RIGHT?
SO,
SOMETHING ABOUT IT JUST PUTS ME AT EASE.

...YEAH.
I THINK I GET WHAT YOU MEAN.

WHAT'S WITH THAT REACTION?
OH...

HUH...?

NO, I'M JUST SURPRISED.
I DIDN'T THINK GENIUSES LIKE YOU HAD MUCH TO WORRY ABOUT...

...YOU THINK I'M A "GENIUS", HUH?

YOU SHOULD SAY THAT TO A REAL GENIUS.
LIKE, SAY, SERIZAWA.

I, UH...
I HAVE AN INTIMIDATING COLLEAGUE WHO JOINED AT THE SAME TIME AS ME TOO...
SHE'S SO AMAZING THAT THEY'RE ALREADY TALKING TO HER ABOUT DOING CHARACTER DESIGN.

AND I'M STILL COMPLETELY INCOMPETENT.

PLUS, MY MOM DOESN'T THINK MUCH OF THIS LINE OF WORK...
AND I'M DOING SOMETHING I LOVE, SO I PROBABLY HAVE NO RIGHT TO COMPLAIN ABOUT THE LOW PAY...

YOU'RE WRONG ABOUT THAT.

HERE'S A WORD OF ADVICE:
FEELING FULFILLED BY YOUR WORK AND GETTING PAID DECENTLY AREN'T MUTUALLY EXCLUSIVE.

SURE, YOU FEEL HAPPY AND FULFILLED WHEN YOU HAVE A JOB YOU LIKE.
AND IT'S PROBABLY NOT EVEN AN EXAGGERATION TO SAY THAT MAKES IT ALL WORTHWHILE.
BUT BEING FULFILLING IS NO SUBSTITUTE FOR ADEQUATE PAY.
北1丁目
EVEN WORK THAT YOU ENJOY DESERVES APPROPRIATE FINANCIAL COMPENSATION.

I DON'T WANT THE PEOPLE WHO GIVE THEIR ALL TO CONTRIBUTE TO THE WORK I DIRECT TO JUST FEEL FULFILLED.

I WANT TO MAKE SURE THEY'RE FINANCIALLY SECURE TOO.

THIS MIGHT BE

THE END FOR STUDIO 7.

Not A Winner

ANIMETA! 03: END

Yaso-chan, thank you so much. If it hadn't been for you, I don't think Eden of the East would have happened. Thank you for recommending Honey and Clover to Director Kamiyama...

MS. UMINO ONCE ASKED IF SHE COULD START CALLING ME BY THE SAME NAME MY COWORKERS DID, BUT...
CRT TV
Honey & Clover
My youth...
I WAS BLESSED WITH MANY OPPORTUNITIES TO MEET HER AFTER THAT TOO.
Around then, Honey and Clover got an anime adaptation, so I got the opportunity to do a little tiny bit of key animation on it.

WELL, AT SOME POINT, SHE STARTED CALLING ME THIS:
YASO-CHAN!
I'm sorry this doesn't look anything like how she draws herself...
YES...
"YASO" IS THE NICKNAME MS. UMINO GAVE ME.
WHAT DO YOU WANT YOUR PEN NAME TO BE?
YASO HANA-MURA.
I LIKED IT SO MUCH THAT I MADE IT MY PEN NAME.

BUT IT WAS AT THAT POINT THAT I LOST MY OPPORTUNITIES TO SEE MS. UMINO.
SPARKLE
I STARTED TO WONDER IF SHE WAS A MYTHICAL MANGA ARTIST WHO LIVED IN THE CLOUDS WHO I'D NEVER BE ABLE TO SEE AGAIN.
I FIGURED THAT SINCE I USED HER NICKNAME FOR MY PEN NAME AND WAS TRYING MY HAND AT MANGA, MAYBE MY FEELINGS WOULD REACH HER EVENTUALLY!
THAT WAS THE THOUGHT RUNNING THROUGH MY HEAD.

BUT THEN, A MIRACLE HAPPENED.
Animator Festival
I MADE MY MANGA DEBUT LAST MONTH!
AND I USED YASO AS MY PEN NAME!
WHOA?!
ABOUT A MONTH AFTER MY DEBUT, I RAN INTO MS. UMINO AT A MOVIE THEATER IN SHINJUKU!
REALLY? I'LL HAVE TO LOOK IT UP AND READ IT.
THANK YOU SO MUCH!
I HADN'T SEEN HER IN OVER FIVE YEARS, BUT SHE REMEMBERED MY NAME...!
Our Wald 9
THE NEXT DAY, SHE SENT ME A MESSAGE ON TWITTER.
Yaso-chan, so this interesting manga I read in a magazine the other day... turned out to be yours!!!
SQUEEEE!
WH—?! WHAAA?!
THANK YOU SOOOOOO MUCH!
Phone
YES, SHOCKINGLY ENOUGH, I WAS THAT YASO.
SOMEHOW, BEFORE SHE RAN INTO ME AGAIN,
MS. UMINO HAD ALREADY READ THE FIRST CHAPTER OF ANIMETA IN MORNING TWO!
AFTER THAT, SHE CONGRAT-ULATED ME WHEN THE FIRST VOLUME CAME OUT.
I'm so happy!
AND NOW, SHE EVEN DREW THE OBI FOR VOLUME THREE! I'M SO, SO, SO THANKFUL!
Special Thanks
• Chica Umino
• Everyone at Anigera Diduuun! (Especially Mr. Tomokazu Sugita and Mafia Kajita)
• Studio TRIGGER (Mr. Otsuka, Mr. Masumoto, and Ms. Tsutsumi)
• Chubu
• Everyone who helped with producing Animeta! and getting it to market
• Kaneda-sama, Tonpu-sama, Uchi no Ace
• All my readers
• Obayashiya
I'm counting on you all for volume 4!

ANIMETA! VOLUME 3
by Yaso Hanamura

Translated by T. Emerson
Edited by Maneesh Maganti
Lettered by Kai Kyou

First published in Japan in 2016 by Kodansha Ltd., Tokyo.
Publication rights for this English edition arranged through Kodansha Ltd., Tokyo.

Find more books like this one at www.j-novel.club!

President and Publisher: Samuel Pinansky
Managing Editor: Aimee Zink
Manga Editor: J. Collis

ISBN: 978-1-7183-5802-7
Printed in Korea
First Printing April 2020
10 9 8 7 6 5 4 3 2 1